"For men and women who have lost a child, *No Child in My Life* offers an important means of sharing grief and letting readers know that they are not alone."

Elisabeth Kubler-Ross, M.D.
author of *On Death and Dying*

No Child in My Life

No Child in My Life

Regina Sara Ryan

STILLPOINT PUBLISHING

STILLPOINT PUBLISHING
Building a society that honors The Earth,
Humanity, and The Sacred in All Life.

For a free catalog or ordering information, write
Stillpoint Publishing, Box 640, Walpole, NH 03608, USA
or call
1-800-847-4014 TOLL-FREE (Continental US, except NH)
602-756-9281 (Foreign and NH)

This book is manufactured in the United States of America.
Cover and text design by Karen Savary

Published by Stillpoint Publishing, Box 640,
Meetinghouse Road, Walpole, NH 03608

Library of Congress Catalog Card Number: 93-83591

Ryan, Regina Sara
No Child in My Life

ISBN 0-913299-93-6

1 3 5 7 9 8 6 4 2

This book is printed on acid-free recycled paper
to save trees and preserve Earth's ecology.

Dedication

*This book is dedicated to my friend Susan, at whose
invitation this project began. This is her book as much as it
is mine. Through her own losses she envisioned a means of
sharing the transformational nature of grief with other
women or men who had lost a child or a
relationship with a child. It was my privilege to be her
collaborator every step of the way, and, therefore, to drink
daily from the same clear Source of wisdom
and compassion that sustains her.*

Together, we remember Lee, who awakens Innocence.

Contents

Preface   *ix*

Introduction   *xiii*

1. No Child in My Life   *1*

2. Telling the Story   *15*

3. It Doesn't Hurt that Much . . . Really   *37*

4. Am I Going Crazy, or What?   *61*

5. No One to Blame but Myself   *87*

6. It's Out of My Hands   *113*

7. It's Not Fair   *137*

8. Is There a Right Choice?   *157*

9. Something to Live for, Again   *179*

10. Ways and Means   *205*

Bibliography and Suggested Reading   *227*

Resource Guide   *233*

Preface

I HAVE NEVER BORNE a child. Twenty years ago, and eight months after I was married, a necessary surgery ended that possibility.

At the time I coped quite well. I was grateful just to be alive, so the sacrifice of motherhood seemed like a small price to pay. My husband was consoling and philosophical. "We really didn't want children that much anyway. Right?" We never grieved.

As the years went on I became somewhat of an expert in the field of grief and loss: working as a Hospice volunteer, counselling the families of dying people, teaching the subject in several colleges and adult education programs, even writing a book that applied the process of grieving to the circumstance of illness or injury. In my classes called "Living with Loss" I listened empathically to the stories of hundreds of grieving men and women. With them I mourned the loss of spouses and close friends, children, relatives, and even pets. I touched my own pain as they described the loss of their dreams, or the loss of identity created with severe depression or illness, or their fears of growing old.

My own story, about the loss in relationship to children, sat on the shelf at a safe distance. Certainly, I told it. Many times, in fact, with all sincerity. But more often than not it sounded dry and lifeless to me. My story remained an intellectual experience, neatly wrapped and packaged. It was something to lend credibility to my expertise, but little more. One foolproof way to deny something is to become an authority about it.

I had always encouraged my students to view loss as an opening into a deeper level of self-understanding, as a doorway to compassion, even as a key to genuine spirituality. And I had done this with other losses myself. But, with perhaps the most pivotal event of my life—the disease that assured my childlessness—there was a gift I couldn't claim because I was yet unable to admit and address the pain and sorrow still connected to it. How could I genuinely witness to the transformational potential of such a loss in others?

Something in me, something deeply feminine, needed to be birthed, and for that I needed a midwife.

With the perfect timing that characterizes the feminine principle in life, my long-time friend, Susan, approached me with the intimate and painful experience of her two miscarriages and the insight this suffering had given her.

"It's hard to remain neutral where children are concerned," Susan confided. "I think it has something to do with the innocence that surrounds them. When we lose a child, therefore—either accidentally or consciously, physically or by the termination of a relationship—besides some sense of emptiness or guilt or fear there is as well a less tangible loss. I think it is a loss of that connection to innocence."

Susan's words touched something in me that triggered tears. I felt a physical yearning and a great wave of sadness. I "knew" in my body the experience of giving birth, even though I had never done so, and I "knew" the joy of holding a child in my arms, awestruck that it had come from me.

Susan catalyzed for me the need to take another level of risk: to cut into the scar tissue that was surrounding my loss; to turn and face again, full on, my own story. That process continues to be one of the most powerful and rewarding opportunities of my life. It changes my way of seeing the world, allowing me to glimpse the sorrow that everyone carries in some form or another. It opens my eyes, also, to the unrelenting courage, perseverance, and strength that others live in the midst of their sorrow.

This expanded awareness is a direct result of allowing myself to grieve more fully. The less I deny, the more I am able to access the full range of human emotions, and on that to build a new foundation for spiritual work.

I am a different teacher now, too—less of an observer and more of a participant in others' lives, allowing others to participate more in mine. Inspired by Susan's vision, that exploration has led to the creation of this book.

Many people supported me in this writing project, and I extend my gratitude to them. I acknowledge the hundreds of students who took my courses in grief and loss over the past fifteen years and who shared their stories, their journalling exercises, their poems and drawings. From them I learned what helps and what doesn't when one is grieving. My special thanks to each of the women and men who agreed to be interviewed for this book. Their honesty was disturbing at times, but their pain and courage were tremendously helpful in sorting out the pieces of my own story. I acknowledge the pioneering efforts of Stillpoint Publishing Company, and particularly Meredith Young-Sowers, for first recognizing the importance of the message and for creating the means to communicate it. I am grateful to my editor, Dorothy Seymour, for her sharp eye and her soft words. I thank my friends in community and each member of my household for their encouragement, generosity, and kindness during the year it took to write and always; and I thank "liars, gods, and beggars"—the rock band whose music keeps me moving. Finally, I thank Jere, my husband and friend, who lives my story with me.

Introduction

THIS BOOK is about human beings and the ways we stumble through our grief and finally fall into healing. It is for those of us who have never had a child and for those who have lost a child or lost a relationship with a child. It is based on the recognition that such a loss can be one of the most deeply painful experiences that a human being ever has to face. Like a devastating earthquake, any loss related to children seems to violate the laws of nature, challenging our basic assumptions about a predictable and benign universe. Grieving such a loss, then, will take time and patience, comfort and courage, and plain hard work as we bear the suffering and set out to rebuild some portion of life again.

Whether we are without children through conscious choice or have "lost" a child by accident, whether that loss is the result of adoption, abortion, custody award, death, miscarriage, the inability to bear a child, or the decision to remain without children; in any of these situations we are called to face ourselves and examine our belief systems. We will mourn the loss—whether we show it or not—because mourning is the natural response to being dispossessed of something that was once rightly ours. (Even animals mourn.) And, depending upon our ways of coping and the meaning we ultimately assign to our loss, our lives will be changed forever, for better or worse.

To tell the stories of our choices and our losses, even if those events happened decades ago, can be profoundly beneficial both for ourselves and for those who listen. A story is a medium for healing. It allows us to clarify confusion, to give voice to silent fears, to confess remorse, to release anger. In hearing the stories of others we are reminded that loss is part and parcel of this great process of human and divine evolution, and that it is possible to transform our relationship to pain, sadness, and loss of meaning from one that leads deeper into death to one that points us in the direction of richer life. Knowing that others have walked these painful and sometimes treacherous paths before will enable us to tap into a source of collective wisdom and solace that can carry us through the most difficult moments, hours, and days.

*   *   *

No Child in My Life is a book of stories—true stories spoken by men and women like yourself who have a child-related loss. It is a book of curves and twists and turns because that is the way the path of healing winds, and these stories testify to that. Most people stumble around looking for the next road sign, feeling as if they're walking in circles, longing for the light of day. Nobody here does it "right"—even the strongest and most intelligent. Losing is hard. It's just hard.

And there are ways to avoid some detours, some dangerous corners. A little guidance and a few warnings can save you precious energy and time. I'll do my best to point out those potential pitfalls.

This book is designed to encourage you to remember your own story of loss, and then to speak it, write it, or simply redefine it for yourself within a new context. The loss of a child, I believe, offers a unique connection to the archetypal feminine principle, present in both men and women. This principle compels us to bear life, to nurture life in all its forms, and to heal life more effectively. The more we appreciate this, the more this principle begins to pervade and characterize our lives. It places our pain in a different perspective, allowing us to extract from it something that actually makes all life more precious. That "something" heals us personally. That "something" promises hope for our world.

Satomi Myodo, a Japanese mystic, knew that a healing of the heart was possible even in the midst of grief. Only by dropping our notions of separation from the cosmos, she affirms, can we find our rightful place within it:

> To know the Way is to know life and to know oneself as an individual at home in the cosmos. It is to see one's rightful position in life, one's belongingness, not in a self-centered way, but in a way in which the infinite interrelationships of oneself and all other beings in the cosmos—both animate and inanimate—are made clear. Becoming free of egotism, one who knows the Way sees things the way they are, rather than how he or she might wish they were. Thus one no longer struggles in vain against the inevitabilities of life, but accepts whatever life may bring, with a calm and peaceful heart. Thus, to know the Way is . . . to live in a truthful, sincere, and harmonious manner.

No Child in My Life

A sound is heard in Ramah, the sound of bitter weeping. Rachel is crying for her children; she refuses to be comforted, for they are no more.

JEREMIAH 31:15

THE FIGURES are staggering. In the United States this year, several hundred thousand women will miscarry a child, many as late as the third trimester of pregnancy, while ten women in every thousand will carry a child to full term only to witness its death within the first year of life. There will be more than 1,175,000 divorces involving a custody decision for 1,045,750 children. Four-hundred eighty-three parents out of every 100,000 will lose a child over the age of a year through illness, accident, or neglect. More than 1,500,000 women (and men) will choose to end pregnancy through abortion, and one out of six couples will learn that they are infertile.

Add to these numbers the millions who will resign themselves to never raising or bearing a child because they never
found a suitable partner or because the biological clock simply got the better of them. The statistics are fast becoming
astronomical, and these are just the beginning. Uncountable
are the masses who will grieve the emotional or spiritual loss
of a "normal" relationship with their children. Think of your
own friends and family members. Can you name three who
have "escaped" with none of these losses? It is a sobering
reflection.

Child-related loss, and the pain that follows it, is universal. If there is one element that unites humanity, binding us
together with a chain of tears, it is our sensitivity to and our
outrage about the sufferings of children. Even if we have
never borne a child, the archetypal image of a child separated from its parents, as we frequently see during times of
war, conjures up a primitive recognition of abandonment,
causes us to cry out in anger at the injustice and connects us
with our own feelings of abandonment and betrayal. Children
belong with their parents. Parents are supposed to love and
care for their children. When this can't happen or doesn't
happen, we all grieve.

Everybody who loses a child in any way, either consciously or by unavoidable circumstance, may experience
grief—whether they acknowledge it not, whether they do it
overtly or not. We human beings are not very different from
some animals. Besides carrying on physical searching
behavior, many animals will become despondent, a sign that
they are mourning the separation from their young.

Suffering and loss are inherent in human life. We grieve
because the world changes around us, and we don't like it.
We grieve because those we love leave us. We grieve
because we know we won't live forever, and neither will our
children. The emotional heart is easily broken or bereaved.
We need only read the newspapers each day to be faced with

new evidence that the human race is one vast fellowship of the wounded.

These reflections, however, are not meant to drive us deeper into pain and depression but rather to open our eyes to the reality of what is. It is very dangerous to deny mortality and to bury the pain of our existence. Appreciating reality can actually be a source of a tremendous potential, the seeds of a flower of compassion. Grieving our own loss connects us to everybody's losses. If we have the sensitivity and forbearance we can tap the collective suffering of humankind. And that is a tangible way of sensing the interconnectedness of all life.

WHAT IS A CHILD IN MY LIFE?

Besides the fact that they are so real that they defy description, children are symbols—of different things for different people. That highly personal and symbolic meaning will play a major role in influencing our choices related to the presence or absence of children in our lives. And those meanings will determine how we grieve the loss of a child.

For many, children are symbols of having made some mark on the world, some way to carry us forth into future generations. They serve as living witnesses to the fact that our lives have been productive. "Ask me about my grandkids," the bumper sticker reads, announcing that at least we have our children and grandchildren to give meaning and purpose to our declining years.

The desire to give and receive love is probably the most predominant association with the presence of a child. At the mundane level, that may equate with the need to have something or someone dependent on us or the hope that our children will provide us with security in our old age. At its exalted level, however, such a desire is selfless, the draw to sacrifice for another, to move into a unique kind of service that transcends those mundane considerations of what is "mine" or what is "owed" me. Having tasted a fleeting moment of genuine love, the kind of unconditional acceptance that one sees in the eyes of a child, it is natural to long for that, and even to structure one's life to recapture it. Birthing or raising a child seems like the most ordinary and obvious way to do that.

For Wendy, a single professional woman in her early thirties, receiving love from a child was transformative. As a volunteer in a New York City foundling home for handicapped children, she gravitated to the most neglected child in the ward. "I knew Christina less than a year," she told me, "but the effect of her presence on my life will never be dimmed." When Christina became seriously ill, Wendy stayed with her. "I remember the profound love that she gave me as she looked into me. I remember thinking at the time that this must be what divine love is all about. Purely ecstatic. There was no need for anything else. No thought of anything else. Just the two of us gazing in worshipful silence at one another."

Having a child of one's own can be a significant milestone in the journey of life—a rite of passage. Carrying or fathering a child serves as a visible, physical witness that one is no longer a little boy or girl. When one becomes a parent everybody knows that not only does one have the potential to fertilize or conceive, one has actually done it, and the proof of that is now living and growing inside a woman's womb.

"Mother" has vast symbolic meaning. It means, at least at the level of the cultural myth if not in reality, that one is a whole woman, a nurturer, a healer, a lover, a creator. "Father" means manhood, provider and protector, lover, and creator too. For a child there is actually no distinction between the mother or father and God. For an adult, feeling and knowing that sense of power, that sense of fulfillment and love, as fleeting or as filled with fantasy as it may be, nevertheless fuels the desire for a child in one's life.

For women especially, the experience of bearing a child is often a profound liberation. Susan, who carried the burden of unworthiness from a childhood of sexual abuse, found a unique sense of self-esteem growing along with her child. For Julie a child meant that she could join the ranks of the "normal" people, doing something that was socially approved, winning the attention she had long sought from her parents and siblings.

On the other hand, with "no child in my life" I frequently encounter the questioning or pitying looks of those who seem to be asking: "Oh, what's wrong with you, or are you just selfish?" For some of us who have no children by choice or accident, that absence, even if we are clear and resolved about it, may symbolize estrangement from many dimensions of life that even our closest friends may take for granted. Even the word "family" may become charged for us, and gatherings of brothers and sisters with their squadrons of healthy kids may be more painful than we care to admit.

When we lose a child or give up our children, we may equate that with failure. "If there was anything I ever wanted to succeed at in my life it was being a Mom. I feel that I have succeeded in failing even this task," said one middle-aged woman who chose to have her children stay with their father because she thought it would mean a more secure life for them. Issues related to children in our lives cut deep, sometimes to the core of our definition of self.

SYMBOLS OF INNOCENCE

> *He who mocks the infant's faith*
> *Shall be mocked in Age and Death.*
> *He who shall teach the child to doubt*

The rotting grave shall ne'er get out.
He who respects the infant's faith
Triumphs over Hell and Death.
                          WILLIAM BLAKE

Children shine with innocence—a primitive sense of trust,
lack of discrimination. They see the world without the boundaries around countries, without distinctions of race or color or
belief system. And that innocence is one of the most compelling
forces in the world. Innocence cuts through the strongest
defenses, and most of us find it difficult to resist the smile of a
child. In smiling back we make a tiny crack in the armor of
rationality and invulnerability that we normally wear.

Children are symbols of life and therefore of hope. We
crave that aliveness that children exude naturally. We need
them as reminders of us. Until they learn to adapt to others,
children have no rules. Seeing the spontaneity, freshness,
unpredictability, and that still-intact sense of innocence and
wonder that a child holds, "grown-ups" can be moved to
remember their own joy, their goals and visions for the
future, their dreams of a life without limits. Touching that
innocence is often compared to touching God, as William
Blake and other poets have so often reminded us. So our
children become our companions and playmates and often
our teachers—ongoing sources of inspiration and help.

But innocence carries more than positive symbolic
value. Seeing innocence, we also realize its opposite: the lack
of innocence, the loss of innocence.

"What are you thinking about?" I asked my friend, a
young Vietnamese performing artist, as we sped through the
underground of Paris several years ago. I had noticed that
she was studying, with a combination of intensity and gentleness, the children who squirmed in the seat across the aisle.

Silence. Atta, a refugee, was prone to moodiness, a
quality that she capitalized on in the development of her solo

art. So I left her to her thoughts and occupied myself with looking out the window, letting myself be lulled by the movement of the train and the bright flashes of color off the billboards in the stations.

Over our meal she broke her silence at last. "I was shaken, again, by the innocence of those children," she began in a tone that revealed how serious this subject was for her. "I study children a lot. I ask myself what is it that they still have now that I have lost . . . precisely. How long will they have this? How will it go away? And why can't I have this again?"

This, for Atta, was no idle conversation but an inquiry into the nature of innocence that literally had implications of life-and-death proportions. As an artist, she felt obliged to understand this precious commodity of innocence and to re-enliven it, or provoke questions about it, for her audience. As she told me her own story, a wrenching tale of separation from her family of origin, her culture, her homeland, it was clear that this subject had never been far from her awareness. She had literally lost everything—except herself. And that was now the only raw material she had from which to create her art.

Over the years that have intervened since that evening I have come to appreciate more fully, as Atta did, that the glimpse of innocence is a sacred jumping-off place. Such an inquiry then becomes a divining rod that seeks out the underground streams of truth that wind far below the surface of all our life activities and that rise occasionally, in bubbling pools, at times when our defenses are down or our perceptions are sharpened. Grieving does that.

Grieving any loss in relationship to a child will force us to engage the subject of lost innocence around every corner. And that engagement will lead us to the heart of the mystery that is life.

NO CULTURAL CONTEXT FOR INNOCENCE

We must start at the beginning, with the fact that we were
all innocent and that we have all lost that to one degree or
another. Even if we were raised by unusually sensitive
adults, life gave us reason to grieve. We saw our toys broken
or our pets taken away. We heard our parents break their
promises to us. We felt the effect of cruelty from other children, and we didn't understand.

Whenever these things happen (for some it is in infancy,
for others later), the slow process of the erosion of our innocence begins. It needs to be this way. Before we can glean
true wisdom we must see the darker sides of life. The natural erosion of some aspects of the innocence of childhood must
be borne if we are to receive our initiation into adulthood.

More often, however, innocence is not eroded naturally
but rather wrenched away, smothered, manipulated, or
seduced by parents or systems that are simply too threatened by the remembrance of what they themselves have
lost. Well-meaning people will unconsciously shame their
children and burden them with undue responsibility, even
from infancy denying them their childhood. This travesty is
enacted every day in a million different ways.

The fact that innocence doesn't get completely washed
out is a testimony to some mystery of the human spirit.
This innate innocence is quite strong and quite resilient.
Miraculously, despite the terrors of our lives, we resurrect
over and over again the freedom, the freshness, and the
wonder.

I believe we live in a culture that devalues innocence
and all that goes along with it. While we definitely pay lip
service to the need to preserve innocence in our children, the
voices of the media, particularly television, together with all
the industries that cater to supplying children with clothing,
food, toys, and entertainment, testify to the opposite stand.

It is so pervasive that we are almost immune to it and sometimes feel the shock only when we encounter a child who is still untouched by it all. But the problem then becomes that such an "untouched one" will soon be ridiculed. Our schools put such emphasis on intellectual mastery, and even sophistication, that innocent children will often look stupid by comparison with their peers.

Yet our schools are not to blame. They are simply reflecting the pulse of the culture in which innocence and playfulness, particularly in adults, cannot be distinguished from naiveté, weakness, and idiocy. I know that I have often curtailed my own spontaneity and childlikeness for fear of ridicule. I know that I am being untrue to myself over and over again for fear of what other people think.

All this cultural emphasis on appearance, on the way we look outside, has actually become more important than the cultivation of the soul. When we encounter one who doesn't fit with the cultural norm of intelligence or appearance, yet still possesses some quality of heartfulness or innocence, as we do in meeting children or some mentally-retarded adults, or in reading stories of encounters with native peoples, we are often touched deeply, perhaps even disturbed.

LEARNING TO GRIEVE, AGAIN

Unless you become as a little child . . .

LUKE 18:17

It was the week after Halloween, and I watched with respect as my friend Maryann, a young mother, explained again to her year-old daughter, Carrie, the fate of the dying pumpkin. "Pumpkins grow, and then people pick them and eat them or use them for jack-o'-lanterns, and then they begin to decay. They go back to the earth. . . ."

Carrie's experience with this pumpkin, Maryann told me, had amounted to an all-consuming event. The child, at one year, wasn't yet speaking in words, but with a series of sounds and facial gestures, which I immediately saw as grief, she clearly communicated her concern and wonderment for the fate of that friendly orange presence that had sat on her windowsill for three weeks and that she rejoiced in watching come to life when her mother lit it every night.

Almost seven days later the child was still asking for it. "Not as much as she had at first," Maryann remarked. "It has been lessening day by day," she told me. Again, as I sat there, the silent observer to this drama, Carrie made the inquiring sounds, and Maryann, as if for the first time, patiently explained the cycle of life and death, retelling the story of the way they had carefully carried the pumpkin to the compost heap, and reiterating that "everything is food for something else." Carrie became silent then, and nodded her head. She had understood completely.

That night, telling the story to another friend, I was aware of a tightness in my chest, a sudden discomfort in my ability to take a full breath. Certainly, it was a tender story, an inspiring one, too, but the reaction I felt was not about that incident alone. I was feeling pain for myself. Then it all fell into place. I saw instantly the huge gap between this child's experience and my own. Faced with one of her first "koans" about the nature of the human condition, Carrie was receiving enlightened input—acknowledgment of her grief and the opportunity to tell her story, over and over and over, while the healing took place. With this simple beginning, Carrie was allowed to witness loss as a part of life rather than as the enemy. She was introduced to the rightness and beauty of the changing seasons and thus to the only constant in life: change. She was encouraged to question birth, growth, aging, decay, dying, and death; she was honored in the expression of her emotions.

What sharp contrast this made to my own story and in the stories of the men and women I had interviewed for this book! How many of us were rushed through our pain—"It's only a bird, now that's enough!" or immediately offered a substitute, another way of postponing inevitable grief—"Don't cry, we'll get another one. Or how about a kitten?"

Because so many of us grew up without role models for the healthy expression of grief, the normal grief that is part of being a human being, we lack the internal permission to access, no less to act out, the depth of our own pain. When we lose something as precious as a child, or a relationship with a child, it is no wonder that many of us shut down or develop unhealthy strategies for coping with this devastating pain. It is also no wonder that we fail to see or hear the grief of the children around us. Without this "seeing" we only perpetuate a nonchalance, if not a downright denial, about the reality and rightness of human pain. And, unless we do something about it, this denial will become the legacy we leave to our own and others' children.

GRIEVING: AN INITIATION INTO WISE INNOCENCE

I experienced the awakening of all these considerations as I looked again at my own losses. For me it has become abundantly clear that in order to grieve, to mourn, and ultimately to heal, I must come out of denial about my own lost innocence.

Loss is cumulative, which means that every loss triggers the memories of every other loss. When my friend Susan lost two pregnancies through two miscarriages in one year she wasn't grieving only for them or for herself in the present circumstance. Rather, that pain drove her back to the memory, and in fact the bodily experience, of another pain, one that nobody could fix—ever. She re-experienced the pain she felt as a helpless child who had no one to turn to when something frightening, something overwhelming, was taking place. Because of those miscarriages she had no choice but to explore more deeply her issues around the incest that had terrified her throughout childhood, arousing feelings and fears that she was still trying to avoid. This painful confrontation, however, was the key to exposing the wound, cleansing it, and ultimately healing it.

Susan is not alone in this. In nearly every interview we conducted for this book, the men and women we talked to made a similar connection. They shared their tears for the losses of their children, or the children they never had, but they admitted humbly that the tears were for themselves, too: tears for the innocent one within themselves who was being neglected, misunderstood, or unexpressed. Losing a child, or facing the pain of such a loss, sends many people to therapy for the first time. "That unlocked a door that had been sealed for decades," wrote one man about his entry into therapy following his custody battle. "It was a painful process, but I mourned for my own divorce from deep parts of myself."

In many ways grief work can give us back our innocence. In this, the most painful confrontation with our powerlessness, in the midst of feeling angry, sad, confused, guilty, we are raw, vulnerable. We are shocked out of the staid conformity of our adulthood, challenged at the level of our predictable defenses and in our attachments to things less than ultimate. When a child is lost, as a reality or as a symbol, we start re-evaluating priorities, and many report that their formerly materialistic goals may suddenly start to transform into spiritual values.

This reconnection to an organically innocent state is not merely the naive innocence of childhood but something I have learned to call *wise innocence*, which is really maturity with innocence still alive. Wise innocence has its roots in the recognition that health, basic goodness, and joy are our birthright. It serves as the foundation for the cultivation of spontaneity and happiness.

While wise innocence is definitely possible to achieve in other ways, grief work is a hard but fast path to that end. I think that the longing for wise innocence is a big part of the emptiness we feel when we lose something precious to us, and that simply naming it as such can be extremely helpful. Knowing what it is possible to discover in the midst of this journey, we may be more likely to recognize it, treasure it, and start putting it to use when we stumble across it on the way.

Grieving the losses related to the presence of children in our lives, even years after the initial event that led to the loss, holds the power to open us to a new relationship with life, with ourselves, and with others. It enables us to create a wedge in that crack in the armor, opening it enough to give ourselves a little more breathing room. With that we take a great stride in this journey towards wholeness.

2

Telling the Story

Our culture is riddled with the loss of feeling values because so many stories go on in the soul but are never heard.

MARION WOODMAN

WHY DON'T YOU just begin by telling us about your loss," Susan and I would invite gently, after the preliminaries and the tea-pourings had settled down. "Start wherever you like, or go back to the beginning, as you wish," I continued, noting how these words alone were often enough to bring tears to the eyes of the men or women who had agreed to be interviewed about the children they had lost or never known.

The tears, I found, were of gratitude as often as they were tears of the recollection of painful memories—gratitude that another human being would care enough to simply sit and listen to the story of their struggle, their confusion, the painful decisions they were called upon to make. I encouraged them to take their time.

Two or sometimes three hours later, as we said our goodbyes, each person thanked us deeply, some with silence and more tears, others with hugs and profuse words, for the privilege of being able to share themselves with us. We had been their witnesses, nothing more. They had guided themselves through their own unique labyrinth of pain, moving closer to their own light with every admission of guilt, of fear, of failure. The aroma of forgiveness and compassion, like a fine incense, permeated the room in which we met and clung to our clothing, our skin, our hair, even if the words of forgiveness were never spoken. Susan and I just sat there, letting our hearts be broken again and again. But the effects of such witnessing, far from being devastating, served instead to energize us. We felt ourselves becoming bonded to these men and women and, through them, with all of humanity.

The tremendous success of current-day support groups for self-help is predicated on the simple fact that telling our stories to an empathic listener, especially one who has undergone a similar loss or one who is unafraid of acknowledging his or her own woundedness, is the first step in breaking the cycle of denial that keeps us trapped in our pain. When someone receives our story without judgment, an opening is created. We then have permission to feel our stories as we tell them: to relive the events that were so horrible, or so frightening, or so sad then, in an environment that is now safe and in fact nurturing. Such a process is like exposing a weeping wound to the sunlight. The rays of sun begin to dry it up, stimulating the healing to take place.

Grieving is a lonely process. It is awfully painful to grasp that no one else, no matter how close that person is to us physically or emotionally, can know the particular texture of our personal suffering, nor can we know another's. The burden of thinking that one bears his or her pain alone often intensifies the pain. Once the silence is broken, however, grieving people find that they are deeply consoled by the realization that each fellow human carries a legacy of pain. It is difficult to deny that survival and even healing are possible when another person, similarly bereaved, sits peacefully in front of you.

We must break the silence. We must tell our stories in order for healing to happen. And that telling can be in the form of speaking or writing. For our purposes, we will first consider the value of the speaking and will introduce later a journal-writing process that can be used alone.

After performing some of the exercises suggested in this book, Katherine, a twenty-seven-year-old woman who mourned the loss of her child through a custody settlement, wrote:

> There is so much value in simply speaking the pain, and
> it is also very healing to write it all out and then hand it
> over to someone else. Sort of like giving it up to God, or
> a higher power. It's not about getting rid of our pain.
> We are not supposed to forget, just acknowledge and
> feel. That simple process brings one to earth—to the
> dust and ashes of feeling "into" a sorrow that everyone
> carries, knowing that we must all reconcile these things.

THE HEALING IS IN THE WORDS

"Words are angels," wrote the psychologist James Hillman, and I find that an appropriate image. Words are alive, and sacred, too. When we speak what is real for us, we sink into the memory of what happened. When we find the words that come all the way up from our toes, the ones that vibrate with truth and emotion rather than simply with some clear intellectual description, something transformational enters into the process of speaking. Blocked energy is released, and despite the pain it stirs up, we feel as if we have been brought to life in a new way. I found in listening to people that telling their stories often provoked surprises. Spontaneously, in the midst of his narrative, Jim, a music-industry executive who had lost two children through divorce, stopped short. "Oh, that explains something. That's a piece I've been missing in this whole puzzle." Speaking does that. It encourages us to "fill in the blanks" and inspires us to remember some of the depths of wisdom that we each possess. Such story-telling serves as a reconnection to our "Source"—our inner wisdom, God, higher power—and to the lost parts of ourselves.

Many times, however, as Barbara, or Robert, or Ruth spoke the stories of their losses, I could hear that they were still detached from parts of it. It was told with a sense of unreality, as if the story had happened to someone else. Sometimes the speaker noted this for himself or herself. "It's like telling about a horror movie that happened for some poor woman. But it's hard to get the message that the woman was me," confided one of our friends. That is precisely why it is important to tell the story many times. That is how we come to start *hearing* it for ourselves. With each narration we get a little closer to finding the "body" to our words. "The more I speak," one woman told us, "the more I feel. The more I feel, the more I grieve. The more I grieve, the more I accept."

As we tell our stories over and over, we also begin to make distinctions, like the distinction between what was within our ability to change and what was not, what we were respon-sible for and what we weren't. Such distinctions build a sense of personal power. We start to achieve some clarity about our decisions, and with that comes clarity about our lives.

THE SAFE PLACE

I recommend strongly that you don't speak to just anybody or everyone about your grief, unless you are ready to be judged as "strange" or self-indulgent, or to be consoled quickly and sent on your way. Many listeners are afraid to hear you out because they fear their own pain, which will be triggered if they acknowledge yours. They want to fix you up before you have even made your own diagnosis.

Ideally, we should speak the truth of our experience to an objective—that is, non-judgmental—witness in a "safe place," like a session with a counselor or a clergyperson or in a self-help support group. The ground rules for many of these groups include no advice-giving and sometimes even no hugging, since this form of touch can easily be used to placate the one in pain. The list of such groups grows daily and can be found in almost every city and even in small towns throughout the United States. (See the Resource Guide at the back of this book.)

Close friends or family members can also be used as witnesses, as long as your experience with them is that they are able to listen well. It may feel humiliating to admit your weakness or your sorrow. You need some assurance that your listener will not use that weakness against you. It must be okay with them that you might curse or swear, perhaps against God, or tell secrets about your father or mother. A "safe place" is an environment in which you will not be hurt or punished for such acts, since those are the very ways in which you move out of denial. The poet Dylan Thomas, in speaking of the impending death of his father, chose words that throbbed with intensity. "Do not go gentle into that good night," he moaned, and then exploded: "Rage, rage against the dying of the light." It takes special courage to witness to another's rage and to offer no cheap solution to it.

My own experience of sharing my grief with caring

friends convinced me of the nurturance and power inherent in such an act.

From My Journal: Today Susan invited her friend Cece to join us for the morning. We met in my office for the purpose of recording my story for the book. Susan typed on the computer and Cece sat with me, asking questions and listening with reverence. It was a warm and nurturing environment, and I felt safe. Later, I read back over the pages of my "testimony." Strong feelings! It also confirmed for me the revelatory nature of this process of simply telling a story to a caring witness. Some of what I read actually shocked me. Even before I started my narrative Susan recorded my string of apologies. I tried to reassure her and Cece, fearing that I would have "nothing new" or "earth-shattering" to share. That confession alerted me to a dynamic of self-deprecation that I know to be common in those who deny grief. "I've told my story before, and even written about it," I said. "I think I understand all the whys and wherefores of my hysterectomy and why I have chosen not to adopt children."

The women encouraged me. They knew that I had accepted my loss intellectually, but, even more than I did, they saw that my body had not yet fully mourned. Something was blocking that.

The more I talked, urged by their gentleness and acceptance, the more I softened. It was a bodily sensation— being kneaded, like dough. Like the way I feel after taking a sauna, or after making love. I felt tender inside, and childlike. And the more they questioned, the more I opened. I touched my grief.

Grieving takes us into the "underworld," which, in the cosmology of the ancient shaman, was both the domain of the terrifying demons as well as the respository of the secrets of healing. In our own day, the "demons" are more likely the strong, sometimes overpowering emotions that are denied expression in polite company. Western culture seems to have set as its goal the burying of all underworld interactions and avoiding them at all costs. And that makes for perversions and for leakages of violence, sometimes uncontrollable violence.

The telling of the story, then, is like a safety valve on a furnace, allowing us to release some potentially dangerous pressure. It is healing in the same way that any genuine confession is healing. What we hide only causes our shame to grow stronger, to change shape, or to root itself more deeply. When we confess, telling our story to a witness, admitting the ways in which our pain has provoked interior violence— feelings of self-hatred, coupled with the desire to take revenge—we find that, rather than alienating or isolating us, our truth causes our listeners to breathe a sigh of relief.

In my own case such confession actually put me into deeper communion and understanding with my friends. It gave my husband an important key into the way and the reason I often react as I do. This inspired greater patience and understanding in him and softened his reactions to my occasional painful outbursts.

Your witnesses will probably feel your rage or sorrow, too, but they will not try to stop it. What they provide, then, is genuine sanctuary in the healing process—like the sacred sanctuary of a church or temple. Such a sacred space invites and draws forth the power of the holy, healing spirit that each being possesses. This spirit is not separate from the natural, unfolding process of life, which will move in the direction of healing once the environment can support it.

A witness is one who remembers for you what you may easily forget about yourself, particularly during a time of great stress: that beneath all the apparent fragmentation, the pain, the craziness, the sense of being out of control, the tears and anger, you are essentially whole; your essence is

one of "basic goodness," as the Tibetan spiritual teacher
Chogyam Trungpa taught; and that wholeness and goodness
are the strongest, most enduring substances in creation!

Deborah reminded me of the power of witnessing. At
age twenty she had decided to give up her child for adoption.
Now, twenty-five years later, she shared how she would be
with another woman in the same position.

> If I had the chance to speak to another woman who was
> planning to do what I had done, I'd just want to hold
> her. I probably wouldn't say much, except maybe, "Oh
> God, I know it's painful." I could share my experience.
> That's really all we can share. We can't feel it for some-
> one else. But it helps just in speaking it and saying,
> "This is what happened for me." Maybe she would see
> something beautiful is possible even through all this
> sorrow.

READING THE STORIES OF OTHERS

This book is the result of a process of storytelling in a safe
place. It contains stories of the grieving and healing of men
and women who have never had a child, or have lost a child
or a relationship with a child—the kinds of stories you
would hear again and again if you were to participate in a
grief support group. Reading their stories, you will be
their listeners, and that will be a confrontation. Their pain
will remind you of your own. Their remembrances of
strength and wisdom will connect you with your own. You
will be their witness insofar as you are able to be a witness
to yourself, a listener to your own story. This challenge to
witness will be an invitation and a help to soften your judg-
mentalness toward yourself, to offer yourself the same

degree of compassion you will be feeling for another. These stories are for you.

As I opened to the grief of the people we interviewed, the hard-packed soil that surrounded my own story of loss was being loosened. For days afterward I started having more specific memories of the events surrounding my hysterectomy. I started to trace back to the events in my childhood that were revealed when I made a decision not to be a mother. Suddenly, I saw a whole new dimension to my grief work. I was not only mourning the loss of motherhood, I was confronting the pain of lost innocence. Another woman's story awakened all this for me. I felt myself embracing her as the tears came washing over me.

When anyone opens his or her grieving process in a real way, and if we are really vulnerable with the grieving person in that process, we awaken the possibility of furthering our own evolution in our own grieving.

TIMING IS EVERYTHING

Grieving and healing don't obey an objective timetable. Elisabeth Kubler-Ross, who pioneered the contemporary movement into conscious grieving, claims that some individuals grieve "hard and fast," adding quickly that the rest of us grieve "hard and slow." As witnesses to our own or somebody else's process, it is essential to honor the timing. Not everyone is ready to feel the full effect of the wound. Denial serves a necessary and compassionate function: the body-mind system needs time to adjust to losses that will affect every aspect of its operation. Mercifully, it will naturally keep some things hidden from itself in an attempt to modulate the shocks. We can do ourselves and others a great disservice by exerting pressure to "deal with it all" too soon.

This is especially challenging when we can see someone's pain so clearly written on his or her face or so deeply
absorbed in the body. We want to help people through that
pain, to relieve it by giving the grieving person an outlet.
Yet we need to tread very softly and respectfully here. A
witness can invite but should never demand. A witness will
trust the wisdom of the soul. If, as in the Twelve-Step
Programs that have evolved from Alcoholics Anonymous,
one is aiming for surrender to a higher power, then one has a
stronger base for trusting the process as it unfolds, knowing
that it has its own timing, its own patterns, its own cycles.

You can trust that timing in yourself as you read these
stories. You can put this book down whenever you've "heard
enough" for one day and pick it up again when you are ready
to take the next turn along your own road. Especially for
those who have few, if any, personal witnesses, this book can
be an invaluable resource, provided that it is approached
gently. Invite yourself, slowly, into these considerations of
grieving.

In the second part of this chapter I will be suggesting a
variety of ways in which you can deal with the painful or
fearful feelings that may arise as you work with this material. It will be important for you to have these tools in your
backpack as you start off, or continue along, in this climb.

WE NEED OUR WOUNDS

The Polish have a common expression that, translated loosely, means: "Life is brutal. It is full of traps."

Once we embark on this path of grieving the wounds of
our lives, particularly the ones that are associated with children, we may gratefully experience some relief almost
instantly. There will be a strong tendency, then, to fall into a

common trap. Wanting more relief, wanting to exorcise all our demons, we may start setting up unrealistic expectations that, with enough work, we will free ourselves from all pain, from all wounds. But that is not the way it works. Wounds always leave scars. We don't forget, we just learn to live with our wounds. That is the way it should be.

We need our wounds! Our wounds are the badges of our engagement in this unfolding process of human existence. We should actually be honoring the wounded, including ourselves, instead of fighting with each other or trying to change them or ourselves forcibly by taking the wounds away. What arrogance! And what a waste of time.

When we tell our stories, something universal is present, because when you come right down to it, everyone is wounded, and everyone's wound is the same wound. It is the wound of our separation from who we really are—or you might say it is the illusion that we are separated from basic goodness, or God. We can therefore use our everyday wounds to take us to this ultimate Wound. Just imagine what the world would be like if people approached one another with that recognition of common woundedness. Once we have felt that ultimate Wound for ourselves, we are inspired and energized to work for and with others in a way that can assist them in feeling it, too. And this is the work of a lifetime.

This book is not about becoming perfect, or raising children free of wounds, because I honestly think that is impossible. Where there is life there will be loss. Rather, this book is about becoming an alchemist, one who has learned to recognize that our demons are also our gods. One who can take the base metal of our wounds and turn it into the gold of forgiveness, compassion, and healing for our own parents, our children, and ourselves.

WRITE YOUR WAY THROUGH GRIEF

Shortly after the death of his beloved wife, the author C.S. Lewis began to keep a journal of his personal grief. It was published in 1963, under a pseudonym, and entitled: *A Grief Observed*. In his own words, Lewis referred to these writings as "a defense against total collapse, a safety-valve," and through this process he came to recognize that "bereavement is a universal and integral part of our experience of love."

My own experience verifies the powerful healing and clarifying nature of journal writing, especially during times of crisis. As a bereavement counselor for a residential hospice program in a large western city, I designed (with the help of my director) a journal-writing process for grieving family members. Once a month for a year following the death of their loved ones the family members received a letter from their counselors. Each letter discussed some aspect of the grief process, presented helpful suggestions and small insights from others who had suffered similar losses, and provided a graduated series of questions for reflection or journalling.

This "writing through grief" process had started years earlier in the college and adult education courses I taught, called "Living With Loss." Journal writing was the core of the curriculum and the one constant for dealing with powerful emotional states or plaguing questions and confusion. Writing became, for hundreds of them, a way to ground their unsettling experiences and the means of immediately accessing inner wisdom.

I have written, in secret, many letters that I never intended to send, just because I needed to express thoughts or feelings that would otherwise have been swallowed. The problem with "swallowing" these things is that they don't digest very well and later often create bigger problems.

Releasing them on paper has helped me clarify what I really wanted without placing my anger, or my pain, deeper into my own body, or onto someone else who was really not responsible. The result has been that even though the immediate process was often painful, the final outcome was a sense of relief, lightness, clarity, and occasionally the very unexpected surprise of joy.

Years after the death of his son, Andy did a series of these journalling exercises and found them extremely useful. He wrote:

> This process of expression, through this medium of writing, has, for me, become a lifeline to a very deep and meaningful part of myself that previously had no discipline. The words and feelings were in there all the time, but without a structured form they just sort of floated around. Reading my own words about what is going on for me helps me see who I am and gives me access to something or someone I've wanted to meet for a long time. "Here you are," I say to myself. "Look at how are you doing, and how you are changing. It's all here in black and white." I'm constantly changing, and I want to keep up with myself. There is a world inside me that lies still largely unexplored, no less shared and appreciated. I want to explore that.

TELLING YOUR STORY TO YOURSELF

It is not always possible or agreeable to use another person for a witness to your process. Yet writing the story of a loss, or speaking it into a tape recorder, is an equally valuable means of mourning. In fact, the composing of poems or songs or prayers of grief to give form to an otherwise unfathomable mystery is an age-old practice, an ancient ritual. Think of the Greek tragedies, the Psalms, the Book of Job. In our own day, thousands of manuscripts are written every year, manuscripts that are never published as books, yet serve their authors as ways of putting their grief and pain into perspective, helping the writer to find some value in an otherwise tragic situation.

Most people will admit that they are much more able to see the truth about someone else's life than they are about their own. We have no trouble advising our best friends to "take it a little easier on yourself." We sometimes have prophetic insight into the ways in which our friends are kidding themselves. (It is so obvious at times that we can't believe they don't see it!) Yet, when it comes to being compassionate with ourselves, we are often completely inflexible. When it comes to admitting that "the handwriting is already on the wall" with regard to our own plans or expectations, we can be completely oblivious. Precisely for this reason, writing becomes a remarkable tool. It allows us to put down in black and white what we *do* see and know and appreciate about ourselves. When we read back what we have written it is often like receiving a communication from a helpful friend, if not a wise elder.

Particular types of journal-writing access the voice of inner wisdom, guidance, and balance that is always present. But this voice is easily obscured by competing factors in the consciousness. As Andy noted above, thoughts and feelings float around without a way to be expressed and seem very disconnected, superficial, confusing. When I actually take the time to start putting them down on paper, especially with some structured format, I generally find that a natural "sorting-out" process begins to take place. The truth begins to rise to the surface. I remember what I have previously forgotten.

I realize that many people find writing a chore and would rather do anything else. It might be encouraging for you to know that even some of the best writers consider their work agonizing, and many claim they wouldn't do it if they didn't have to in order to remain sane. One writer, Gene Fowler, put it this way: "Writing is easy. All you do is sit staring at a blank sheet of paper until the drops of blood form on your forehead."

So you're in good company if you feel some reluctance to write. My experience in teaching these methods to hundreds of students in courses about grief and loss is that a little bit of structure goes a long way in helping resistant writers get started. And once started, most people are amazed at the ease with which they can keep going and the rewarding feelings they have when read over the results.

If you do nothing else, however, at least read some of the sample questions that will be offered periodically throughout the book as ways to inspire further journalling. Instead of writing down your answers, simply allow yourself a few silent minutes to think about what you might say in response. I think you will find yourself dealing internally with the issues in a way that can be beneficial.

Another form of reluctance that people occasionally cite is the fear that writing will bring up the pain again, "only making things worse." And that is partly correct. Writing your story, just like telling it, always stirs the embers of your pain, even years after the loss. But the incorrect assumption of this excuse is that feeling the pain means that things are getting worse. It is our experience that this is not the case. Only by facing our pain do we heal it. The "starters" for journal-writing offered here are each designed to help you clarify your thinking, release some of the emotional build-up you have been accumulating, and most of all inspire you to remember your own strength and the depth of your internal wisdom.

BRINGING YOUR WORDS TO LIFE

Writing requires an involvement of the body. You have an instrument in your hand: a pen, a pencil, a crayon, a type-writer or computer keyboard. Translation from thought to paper requires that other neural pathways be stimulated. And the more "parts" of yourself that become involved, the more possibility there is for giving "body" to your words.

"I lost the chance to be a normal mother, of normal kids, in a normal family," wrote one sorrowing mother whose son was diagnosed as severely learning-disabled and whose daughter, a diabetic, is at age eleven rapidly going blind. Her narrative was at first clear and rational, her handwriting neat and tight. Yet a few sentences later she was using the writing to pour out some of the countless hurts that she has to deal with from day to day. "The reactions of people at large have been so grossly insensitive and hurtful that I have a ball of RAGE inside me," she continued, her writing becoming more unrestrained as she spelled out the word "rage" in large, bold, capital letters.

It is common for the writing to take on a life of its own and to take us into areas of expression that we have previously not allowed others to see. Yet, because we can stop at any time, and primarily because there is an inner wisdom that will guide us in the amount we can deal with at any particular time, writing for ourselves can be a genuinely safe place.

Writing is not simply a form of "catharsis"—that is, a purging or release. More accurately, it is a "cathexis"—an interiorization of pain as a means of building a matrix, an internal structure for personal transformation.

In her powerful book, *Leaving My Father's House*, Marion Woodman, a Jungian analyst, reinforces this idea that one's story can be the foundation for one's evolution. She writes:

> In finding our own story, we assemble all the parts of
> ourselves. Whatever kind of mess we have made of it,

we can somehow see the totality of who we are and recognize how our blunderings are related. We can own
what we did and value who we are, not because of the
outcome but because of the soul story that propelled us.
That story is our individual myth."

START HERE

Just as Susan and I invited the people we interviewed for
this book to tell us about their losses, I invite you to do the
same. Use me as your witness as you begin to write, speak,
or simply think about your story. Begin at the beginning, or
start wherever the strongest point of focus, or the strongest
pain, is right now.

Write about what you have recently gone through or
are just starting to discover. Write about your memories
that are stirred as you have been reading the stories of others in this book. Write about your most pressing fears for
yourself or others, or the questions that hound you, or your
sense of being out of control. Any of it, or all of it.

Write your story in the form of a letter to your best
friend, or to yourself as your own best friend. You probably
won't send this letter out, so don't burden yourself by having
to do it "right." We have found that writing a letter is a
great way of tricking yourself into writing when you are otherwise sure you can't write.

Write to your best friend about the loss you are currently going through. Comment on the overall state of
your life right now. You may want to mention your percep-
tion of your health, your ability to handle the stresses that
your loss has brought about, your concerns for your other
children or family members, your performance on the job or
in your social or volunteer activities. In short, write about

anything that is important or troubling for you right now.

"Dear Amy," wrote one student to her best friend, "As I sit down to write to you I am aware of the difficulty and pain involved in bringing my innermost thoughts, feelings, and experiences to light. How can I tell you about the shock of losing my baby, of having to be 'only one' again? Is there any way you can understand the way my dreams, my plans, and my fears, too, died along with the baby? The death of the fear brought some relief. The death of the baby and the dreams brought pure pain and emptiness. . . ."

As she continued her writing, this woman raised numerous questions. She also witnessed to the creation of meaning within herself. "I have been brought face to face with the punishing God of my childhood and have battled with that one. 'He' is a sham. A real God, however, is beginning to show her face to me at last. . . ." She noted how many tangents the writing was taking her on, yet she put them, too, into perspective. "It is impossible to write about my loss without disclosing many experiences that appear to be unrelated to the subject matter, because these events have made me who I am, have determined how I respond to and perceive all that occurs in my life. My grief is inextricably interwoven into the fabric of my life. Thank you for 'listening' to all of it."

The story of your grief may be one letter long, or it may take chapters to explore. But, especially if you are a reluctant writer, it is initially helpful to give yourself a time and space limit so that you don't get overwhelmed at the prospect. You can always write another letter tomorrow! In fact, that's the whole idea. Let your letter-writing become a correspondence. Write your letter on one day, and the next time you write have the letter be *from* your best friend. There are so many voices or subpersonalities within ourselves that it is generally no problem for people to access more than one of them.

Whenever you have completed one writing session, take the time to read back over what you have written. Feelings may develop. Tears or sensations of anger or fear may well up. The way to capitalize upon this dynamic energy for healing is to go one step further in the writing process: the step of temporary synthesis. To do this you simply record: "As a result of writing and reading over this letter I am aware...."

Jane, another student of mine who had suffered the loss of a child, responded in this way: "As a result of writing this letter I am aware that the pain of my loss will never completely leave me, but as long as I grieve my son he is still a part of my life, and I would never trade the pain for the memories."

Terry, a young man, wrote: "Appreciation is one of the largest factors that comes into play for me in doing this type of journalling. I am getting a chance to appreciate myself in ways that I have not done before."

HOW TO WRITE RIGHT

If you decide to use this process as you engage the rest of this book, remember that this writing is for you. Write as if no one else will ever read it, even though you may find that you create something that you will want to share. Your writing might actually be of service to others. I know it is extremely valuable for people who are newly bereaved to read that others have walked this hard path and survived the journey.

So, as you write, be honest. Dare to admit in your writing what you are afraid to admit to someone else because you think it is trivial, or stupid, or humiliating, or sinful, or inappropriate. Get it off your own chest. Let the writing be a form of confessional for you. You can always create a ritual for burning your writing if you want to safeguard your secrets, offer them to God, or signify them solely as a gift in honor of your own personal growth and maturing.

On the other hand, as you write, don't burden yourself with being completely honest. Since we are all struggling to know what *is* truthful for us, writing things out will help you even if you are unsure whether you believe them or not. This is part of the healing process. Many times, we don't know what we are feeling; we just know we feel bad. Writing helps us clarify thoughts and feelings.

Try to work quickly, and avoid reading over your work until you feel complete. This is to discourage self-editing due to self-judgment as you write or create. Most people are amazed at how easily they can express themselves when they put the critic to rest for a while.

Challenge yourself with different modes of expression. If you write only letters, switch for a day and put your thoughts and feelings into poetry, or use crayons or colored markers to draw a picture of what your grief feels like on any particular day. If you generally use descriptive writing, try writing your feelings and thoughts as a dialogue between two people, two different aspects of yourself. All these methods and more will be explained further in Chapter Ten.

Do date all your work. If you are like me, you will find it interesting and encouraging to be able to chart your progress.

Finally, however you choose to write, avoid trying to do it "right." Journalling is often not neat. But, then again, life is not neat, and your journal will be a reflection of your life process. As Natalie Goldberg, a brilliant writer and writing instructor, put it: "Just write, just write, just write. In the middle of the world, make one positive step. In the center of chaos, make one definitive act. Just write. Say yes, stay alive, be awake. Just write. Just write. Just write."

TO NON-WRITERS

Don't hold back from reading on, even if you decide not to write, for the process of grieving will be going on anyway, and the worst thing you need at a time like this is to burden yourself with any unnecessary guilt because you're not following my directions. Forget that.

HOW TO READ THIS BOOK

The chapters that follow are designed and arranged to present you with a self-directed course in grieving your loss. Either read the book from cover to cover or turn to sections that you need most at any particular time. Although each chapter contains one or more stories of particular types of child-related loss—through abortion, or custody, or infertility, for example—the wisdom, inspiration, and practical good sense that these men and women share is universal. So, regardless of the type of loss you suffer, these stories should speak to you. The confusion and ambivalence, for instance, that frequently characterizes loss through miscarriage is present in some degree in every kind of loss.

Each chapter, moreover, has suggested journal-writing entries that will be useful to consider, whether you write about them or not.

3

It Doesn't Hurt that Much . . . Really

IT HAPPENS in different ways. You may discover it your-self, or you may hear it from somebody else. Sometimes people sit you down, take your hand, and look all serious and concerned but kind and even smiling. Then they tell you the thing that you can't afford to hear because it's beyond your comprehension. The thing that happens only to somebody else, but now they're saying it to you. That unthinkable thing you've had bad dreams about and pre-tended couldn't be true. But here is this person, this doctor, or this nurse, or this friend, mouthing words that you can't really hear because it's as if you're all in some strange movie, or maybe you're dreaming, so why can't it just be over? "What are the options?" you hear yourself asking, and none of them sounds like the one you want. You want your baby; or you want your life as it was before any of this happened. You just want to be be normal—and happy again.

When something this big threatens to overwhelm you all at once, the body-mind mercifully shuts down, even for a moment. Shock does that. It suspends us in a temporary state of disbelief. It may even project us into another reality, or back into a fantasy. We need this suspension of reality. It's our way of surviving. Denial is a necessary protective mechanism, giving the organism time and space to tap the energy it will need to cope. A deep sigh and a cry of "No!" may be the body's way of taking a complete breath.

Sometimes the shock is really an afterquake, something that comes only after years. A child passes you on the street, or you wake up from a powerful dream, or a close friend gives birth and is telling you the details ecstatically, when all of a sudden something inside you "breaks"—something you've been holding but couldn't look at, something you've been hungering for but couldn't name. Denial wears many different masks, and it cracks naturally, in many different ways, if we're lucky.

The problem is that denial sometimes gets to be a habit, one we don't even know we have. What worked to keep us alive in the heat of battle can become a daily strategy, one that we fall back on for safety or for the comfort of familiarity. Scared by strong emotion in a relationship? Well, just shut down—again. That's when denial starts to drain us subtly. If it goes on for years it can rob us of life, of health, and certainly of happiness.

It's tough, this process of healthy grieving. Yet we must face the reality of our losses if we are ever to mourn them adequately, integrate them into the fabric of our lives, and then move on. That grieving process requires us to walk the fine line between repression, on the one hand, and necessary self-protection, on the other; between the frank expression of emotions and the over-indulgence in our pain. This is no easy task. We will need help along the way, from those who have walked the path before and can assure us that there is an end to our suffering, those who can assure us that while life will never be the same, it can be okay. Really.

A GRIEF-DENYING CULTURE

A number of years ago I lived for a period of nine months in India. On occasion I spent a few hours sitting in the cremation grounds, which are located by the rivers in almost all the large cities. Here I watched with a mixture of fascination and horror as each grieving family placed the corpse, wrapped only in a fabric sheet, upon the wooden pyre. Chanting mixed with mournful cries when the attendant lit the straw that soon ignited the logs and branches under the body. Here, in the midst of the ritual of death, I frequently observed a gang of young children performing their own rituals—games like "tag" or "follow the leader"—weaving themselves, laughing and shouting, through the crowds of mourners. No one seemed to be bothered by this contrast, or even notice it, except me. These children were not strangers to loss. Raised in a culture where death, disease, and aging, as well as birth and healing, were not separate from everyday life, they were at home here.

How different this situation is from my own! I live in a grief-denying culture that locks away the "crazy," the old, the sick, the deformed. It makes a secret of sex, of birth, and certainly of death, which few are privileged to witness. In doing this the culture cheats me out of half of life. It often inspires me to feel crazy, too. Who wouldn't, when everything in the environment is attempting to convince me that things will be just fine if only I will "buy this . . .

use this . . . move here . . . watch this . . ." or "smile and think positive"? In encouraging me to deny my pain and to forget my losses quickly, it has also trivialized, and thus denied, my pleasure as well.

Ours is a culture that supports the collection of and the grasping onto things and people and circumstances that promote security. But life, the natural world, doesn't work that way. Nature cycles through: conception, birth, growth, diminishment, death, renewal, rebirth. In the process (which it is) there is illness as well as health. There is weakness along with strength. There is loss as there is gain. Out of selfishness, ignorance, and fear, however, many of us don't want to hear that. We desperately want to believe that life will have a happy ending, that the good guy will win, and that we'll all live happily ever after. And in some ultimate sense this is all probably true. But when a situation of loss arises, that ultimate sense is usually far from our current reality. When we lose a child, in any way, we hurt. We suffer. Often, we don't know where to turn or what to do.

I believe that in many ways it's harder today to "lose" than it was even a few generations ago. I am not surprised that we deny loss as we do. Our own grandparents probably had a much more organic connection to the flow of life than most of us will ever know. They saw birth and death with fewer shields of protection. In our day, however, one must work hard, consciously, to keep touch with the facts of existence. It is so easy to fall into the consensus trance that the environment must be controlled—for instance, that heat or cold must be dominated by air-conditioning or heated automobile seats. The media, too, plays its role in this conspiracy against reality. They give us just enough data to enable us to sense some slight control over the events in the world around us; they provoke some superficial catharsis that screens the truth that we are genuinely powerless in the face of most of these forces.

Even well-meaning people participate in this denial of loss. They will try to comfort you, hoping to remove your pain. "Think of the bright side of things," they might say. "You can always have another child." Or "Why don't you adopt?" as if that would heal the wound. Usually, however, we find ourselves feeling annoyed, violated, even enraged by such comments. Most of us have already tried, very hard, to think of the bright side, and have become extremely frustrated in the process. That type of thinking, moreover, becomes a form of denial. Susan, who suffered several miscarriages, told me that she actually had to fight with her "well-wishers." "Don't take my pain from me, I need it for my growth," she would say. "It is too important for me now."

A similar example was portrayed powerfully in the movie "Star Trek V." An intergalactic being, referred to as "God," was apparently offering people an existence free of pain and loss. Captain Kirk, in typical fashion, boldly challenged the temptation to settle into heaven or utopia. In an emotionally-charged scene, an enraged Kirk confessed that he did not want his pain removed, that he needed his pain, and that there was value in feeling it.

The audience of "Star Trek V" approved of Kirk's stand. Yet in daily life, how many of us are ready to make a similar declaration? To walk into a process that we know is going to take us down to "the depths of hell" to wrestle with the painful demons we will find there—that is madness, according to the culture in which we live. Yet experience teaches me that if we do not meet these "demons" at the time, they will cycle around and confront us later. In the meantime, we may pay an exorbitantly heavy price.

*   *   *

It was the first day of the new college semester. I was teaching the course "Living with Loss," which I had taught every fall for the past seven years. Sitting before me, looking embarrassed and uncomfortable, or enthusiastic and eager to get underway, were forty adult students. A quick glance around the room showed the group to be quite typical: a few young people probably in their early twenties; a few seniors; most of the rest in their late thirties or early forties. One man, two men . . . was that all? A second glance confirmed it. Thirty-eight women and two men. It had been like this every term, year in and year out. "Who is helping our men through their grief?" I reflected sadly to the group a few weeks later, after the class had bonded.

"Oh, don't you know by now?" one of the males chimed in. "*Men* can't lose." The room got very quiet as Dave continued, good-naturedly but with an edge of cynicism. "For most of us our whole lives have been about winning: winning favor, winning a job, winning a woman's affection, winning a promotion, winning some great kids, teaching our kids to win at school and at sports, winning the wars, winning . . . , well it should be apparent that a man can't possibly relate to a course called 'Living with Loss.' Maybe you should change the title and see what happens."

The women shook their heads knowingly and sadly. "It's that way with my husband," remarked Rose, a short, well-groomed woman with grey hair who sat close to the front of the room. She was absorbing every word spoken in class as if each was a life raft in a stormy sea. "I would give anything in the world to help my husband break through his pain. He's lost so much in his life—his parents, our thirty-year-old son— and his sister died just last year. Each time it's as if he just pulls the curtain down tighter over his feelings. I'm just so afraid he'll never open it again. Our relationship is dying." She coughed discreetly behind her handkerchief and brushed away the tear that was escaping down her cheek.

Within moments the expected litany began, one woman after another speaking her story of helplessness when faced with the grief of her husband, her son, her father. Soon I felt the room filling up with a vast army of spectres, the lost spirits of their men. Not dead. Just confused. Feeling powerless. Desperate for assistance but not knowing how to ask for it, how to receive it, or how to use it.

It's the thing same every year.

Our culture promotes a taboo against real feeling, and that is certainly understandable. Feeling equals vulnerability, and in the minds of many, vulnerability equals weakness. We don't want to lose. To win, then, likely means armoring ourselves against the pain—through denial or through distraction, usually with some form of addiction. And we have become a nation of addicts.

Real feeling actually turns our world upside down, challenging our polite plans and structures, revealing the petty substitutes for raw life that we have let satisfy us. And yet this challenge can be a tremendous boon. Grieving people frequently speak of their enlightened worldview: the way their pain has given them such a different set of priorities, a different vision of what is important. This new vision amounts to the disassembling of the ego, a death to the "self" that has been known, a step off the edge of the safe pier into the uncharted waters. No wonder there is such a taboo against genuine grief. Carl Jung said that we create our neuroses because we do not have access to our real suffering.

China Galland, author of *Longing for Darkness*, experienced a transcendent understanding of suffering during a state of intense physical pain.

> The voice inside the mountain speaks to me, tells me
> again not to be afraid, tells me that there is only love
> in the world. Our choice is to be in love or to be in
> fear. But to choose to be in love means to have a
> mountain inside of you, means to have the heart of the
> world inside you, means you will feel another's suffer-

ing inside your own body and you will weep. You will have no protection from the world's pain because you will know it as your own. You will understand that this pain is your own because you are not separate, from life, or from anyone or anything else. But you will fall into a forgetting. You may die before you remember. You will forget that you know this, again and again. Do not be afraid. The body remembers, it never forgets. It is your own knowing that you hide from and do not know.

HOW WE DENY

When I awoke from the surgery that took my uterus and ovaries, there was no doubt that something serious had happened. But, at the time, I was so relieved that I didn't have cancer that I couldn't consider the implications of the operation. So I occupied myself, in the days that followed, going along with whatever my surgeon or nurses told me to do: the perfectly compliant and unquestioning patient. Of course, I knew that a hysterectomy meant that I couldn't bear children—but, hey, I was alive, wasn't I? This was no time for complaint.

In the years that I have worked with grieving people I have learned some important lessons about the way denial shows up. I have learned that there are three primary ways to deny:

1. We can deny the circumstances completely or deny our responsibility in them.
2. We can deny the seriousness or permanence of the situation.
3. We can deny our emotions.

We deny the circumstances when, for instance, we ignore symptoms and refuse to initiate medical tests. When we fail to use birth control, we deny responsibility for childbirth. Even men and women far past adolescence, "adults" who know better, often allow themselves to fall into the trap of magical thinking when issues of sex and possible pregnancy are concerned. "I had never gotten pregnant before, so I just assumed that I couldn't," or "We had sex only once," they say with amazement. Even though there are many exceptions, the massive number of unwanted pregnancies and abortions are a testimony to a cultural denial of what it means to be a responsible adult. We don't want to see the simple facts of life as applicable to us. And when the facts are on the table we will often want to shuffle away the evidence as quickly as possible. "I thought if I just kept working, doing my usual jobs every day, that it would go away," admitted one woman who guessed that she might be pregnant when her menstrual period didn't occur as usual.

Denial may mean putting away the whole issue as if it didn't happen. But usually that approach is short-lived because the physical evidence starts to show up: a woman's body changes, or the child gets sicker, or the bleeding gets heavier. More common, and more deeply rooted, are the types of denial that reject the seriousness or permanence of the situation. When a man surprises his wife with the news that he's had a vasectomy (as one of the women we interviewed told us her husband did), that's a form of denial.

When a man demands that his spouse receive an abortion and then leaves her alone to handle it for herself, that's a form of denial, too. A class member named John, then forty-four years old, told us:

> When I learned of my wife's first pregnancy I felt
> nothing. I had little or no sensitivity at the time. I
> was twenty-four years old and really thought only

about myself. So I insisted that she get an abortion. I actually forced the issue upon her, with no appreciation of what her feelings might be. I wasn't in touch with my own feelings, so naturally I couldn't be there for her or anyone else. I was a machine. She was never the same after that. My anger and aggressiveness just blew her out of the water. She never wanted an abortion. I knew that, but I couldn't admit it. She was a beautiful girl.

The remorse around these issues is always there for me now, as a reminder.

Carol's remorse was similar:

When I left Janie's father it wasn't "cleanly." He had been present at her birth and bonded strongly with her at the moment of first contact. We worked at home, so he was with her almost constantly. He adored her, and she adored him. In my running-away panic I didn't take that into account. As we settled ourselves on the plane, headed to a new life in Oregon, Janie, at only seven months old, sat up, looked out the window and screamed "No!" Only then did I get what I'd done, but only for an instant. Over the years I've had to work continually at peeling away the layers of denial and sentiment around my child, myself, and her father.

By far the most common form of denial is the failure, or inability, to allow oneself to feel the emotions that come along with a painful loss. "You've got to be willing to feel the feelings rather than push away what is going on," commented Michelle in speaking about her divorce and the subsequent loss of her son to drug abuse. "As hard as it is to feel these things, it's better than remaining dead. I thought for years that my ex-husband and I had made a good parenting team.

But that wasn't so. When I finally began to see how messed up we were, that was hard to admit. I'm sure it was my fear of feeling more guilty. But I had to look it in the face. I had to let myself get angry, and cry, and feel terror, too, before I could feel the courage and the hope. Now I work with all of it."

THE HIGH COST OF THE FAILURE TO GRIEVE

It is staggering to realize the price we have paid as individuals, as a culture, and as a world community, for the inability or unwillingness to face, deal with, and resolve our grief around children. The renowned psychologist and author, Erich Fromm, asserted that the inability to grieve lay directly at the root of the increase of violence in society.

For many of the men and women whose stories are related here, the symptoms of unexpressed grief are not overt violence toward society but rather violence in the form of illness, self-negating habits, mistrust of others in relationships, and generally low self-esteem.

The stress of unresolved grief robs life of color. "A hum-drum, staid, wallflower mood," one woman labelled it. At the age of twenty Andrea had given up her child for adoption and was still, at age fifty, carrying the wound of shame and guilt. "I have great difficulty in keeping a long-term relationship with a man and find an inability to trust other women," she said sorrowfully. I noted the lacklustre condition of her hair and the style of dress that made her look twenty years older than she was.

With Robert, a father who had lost the custody of his three sons, the patterns were different but self-destructive nonetheless. Until very recently he carried the failure of his marriages as a cross that he assumed he had to bear alone. "I couldn't talk to anyone about it, especially not other men," he sobbed during a particularly touching moment in his interview with Susan and me. Now in his forties, Robert has had a string of affairs with women that have lasted a few months at most. He admits that years of his life were lost to patterns of denial and irresponsibility, punctuated by a handful of serious accidents.

My years of experience in the field of holistic health and wellness have convinced me that disease is never the result of one factor alone. Rather, illness (and that includes accidents and emotional illness as well as physical illness) has multiple causes. Influences in the mind, body, spirit, emotions, genetics, environment, and maybe even astrological configurations determine those who get sick and when that illness will occur. Nonetheless, it is clear to me that our failure to grieve any trauma adds an additional stress to the body-mind, weakening the immune system and making us more susceptible to disease, injury, and depression. I have also observed that people often create situations of sickness, weakness, or failure so that they will look and feel as bad physically as they already feel emotionally and psychically. When that happens, they experience a huge but covert sense of relief, for now there is a reason for the previously unendurable, unfaced pain. And for many, sickness and accidents become a form of ongoing punishment for the "crime" they still hold themselves accountable for, as well as a way to keep forgetting their basic goodness.

The literature about co-dependency, addiction, sexual abuse, and other forms of childhood trauma is filled with similar stories. When we don't grieve our losses directly, we create an infinite number of unhealthy, but often effective, short-term strategies to dissipate or distract ourselves from the anger, the fears, and the sadness that eat away at us. Some become addicted to substances like alcohol, tobacco, or food, which lull the consciousness into a place of forgetfulness or false security. I identify readily with the notion of excitement or adrenaline addictions (which I like to call drama addictions). I have repeatedly found myself creating a circumstance with a level of intensity that is directly proportional to the degree that I am in need of grieving.

It is heartbreaking to witness a once-solid love relationship breaking up because one or both partners are unable to recognize or handle the symptoms of unresolved grief in themselves or in the other. It is more devastating to see these symptoms—anger, confusion, obsession with fear—vented on the children.

Barbara, at age thirty-six, had successfully managed, without surgery, a pre-cancerous condition in her uterus. As we interviewed her about the emotional estrangement she frequently felt toward her children, we explored the connection between her sense of loss and her previous physical condition. Barbara told us about the grief work she had started. It included the telling and re-telling of the story of her own losses. As she spoke to us Barbara cried often—something which she had never been able to do until recently. She was laughing more too, she admitted. It was obvious that in blocking off her feelings of intense pain she had also blocked off the possibility of joy. In gaining the courage to look at her wounds, Barbara also empowered herself to look at her gifts. Lee Lozowick, a contemporary spiritual Master of the Baul tradition, in speaking about the necessity of facing one's pain, said, "In order to experience the highs fully you must also experience the lows fully. And the degree to which we delve deeply is the degree to which we can soar into the upper realms."

MARY'S STORY

Many typical examples of denial are highlighted in Mary's story, which is presented here at length, as she told it to us. But her story is much more than a series of examples. Mary's story is a testimony of a young woman's pain and courage in her struggle to make the right decision for herself and her child.

We are up against some powerful denying forces and
some shaming archetypes when we decide to give a
child away. In the Middle Ages, when a woman didn't
want to raise a family, she was considered to be a
witch. So I guess it's understandable that we find it
hard to feel peaceful about such a decision.

I left home at eighteen and went to art school in
England. I didn't know much about sex and was actually
quite embarrassed about it. (My mother had told me
that babies came because people got married.) But I
wanted somebody to care about me, and in short order I
had a boyfriend who moved in. By the time I got around
to getting contraceptives from a clinic in London, my
next period never came. I was already pregnant.

For months I was in denial about my pregnancy.
That's how naive I was. I considered myself an intelligent woman, but in this regard I just figured something would "happen" so that I wouldn't have to deal
with it. It was as if I would wake up one morning and
this frightening dream would be over. When I finally
faced up to it, though, I was four months along. Some
college friend had given me some drugs that were
supposed to abort, but I just got sick from them.
When I saw the doctor, I learned that it was too late
to have an abortion.

This doctor was actually very encouraging. "Babies
aren't really much trouble," he said. And I was so
needy for any kind of attention, and his words were
honestly the first positive support I had gotten for my
condition, that I actually felt happy at the prospect of
being a mother. Just prior to all this I had been
extremely lonely and had felt so cut off from my family. But now, and at several points throughout the
pregnancy, there was a sense of rightness about the
way things needed to be. The process of life within

me was generating a belief in something benevolent even in the midst of my intolerable pain.

I knew my boyfriend wouldn't like my being pregnant, and I was right. When I told him that I was carrying his child he flew into a rage, hit me in the face, and swore that the baby would never be born. (Talk about denial!) He never called the baby anything but "it."

Things got worse after that. I was twenty years old, plagued with guilt, and had no real maturity to build on for what was happening to me. Most of the time it seemed that whatever I did in my life had some weird failure about it. Whatever decisions I made I was damned if I did, damned if I didn't.

So I reached out to my mother. I flew back to the States. But all this came as such a great shock to her that it was actually more humiliating to me. Mother tried to convince me to give the child up for adoption. In a rage one day she told me, "We're not people from Appalachia"—her way of saying that I might be "white trash," but she certainly didn't want that known in her circles. I was so extremely lonely in that environment that I went back to England to have the baby there.

Luckily, the Social Services in England at that time were very good, so I was well taken care of. I can still remember the name of my welfare person, a kindly woman who was really there for me. She encouraged me to take care of myself, since I was evidently neglecting that and feeling very victimized by the whole thing. I had no real close friends or a support system. It was such a painful time that even today the memories are hard to recall. Needless to say, I didn't go back to my boyfriend.

The baby, a girl, was born in late June. Labor was induced, and she came quickly. I named her Lily.

It was my intention to be a single parent and to keep on with art school, and so for the next seven months I was with her. But it was very hard, and the longer it went on the more desperate I felt. The whole experience of having a child proved to me that I was unworthy. I had suspected it all along, but this was the clincher. Now I was convinced that I had done something wrong and bad and that, because of my own selfishness and unwillingness to sacrifice, I had inflicted my curse on someone else. I knew then that Lily didn't have a chance with me. I was going down for the third time, and I didn't want to take her with me.

Social Services had always kept the door open to adoption, so I called and told the woman that I thought it would be best for my child if I gave her up. I knew it was the right decision. But it was so hard. I cried so much.

I had knitted her a teddy bear, which she really loved. So, when she went, on that cold night in January, the bear went with her. I was in shock for a long time after that. I couldn't really feel anything.

A few weeks later the welfare person gave me a few pictures of her, and she looked really happy. That was the last time I saw her.

It wasn't over for me, though. Not long after, I started having emotional breakdowns, and the doctor put me on Valium and Librium. The situation was just too much for me to handle. He recommended that I go to the local mental health hospital for a rest, and, lost as I was, I followed his advice. But it turned out really bad. That's when I guess I hit bottom. I was there only for a weekend, but during that time I wanted to leave several times, and they wouldn't let me. I couldn't get out until my doctor returned from vacation. It was horrible. The staff treated all the

patients the same: as disenfranchised human beings.
I made a decision then and there that no matter how
dark it got, I was never doing that again.

I punished myself a lot for what had happened. My
anger would come out in self-abuse—overeating, a
sense of detachment and hatred for my body, a constant barrage of put-downs of myself for being irresponsible, untrustworthy, unlovable. It's almost been
a banner I've carried. Quite systematically, I avoided
creating relationships that worked. I just didn't have
the tools that would make them last.

I shut down my feelings so strongly that denial just
became a way of life for me. And of course my parents
never mentioned it. For them it is still as if it never
happened. Their way of handling things is to deny
them until the situation becomes totally desperate.

I guess that's what I did, too.

MARY'S GRIEF PROCESS

Mary continued her story, explaining how she worked
with her grief over many years.

I have never had any more children. It's a complicated issue for me still. On the one hand, I wanted to be
around children; I even ran playgroups and taught
school for a number of years because I was so drawn
toward children. Another part of me was thrown into
turmoil when women who were close to me had children of their own. I didn't know how to be with them,
since I still had such an immense pain that I couldn't
heal, and that is what finally brought me into therapy.

I had so much shame. Not just around having my
child, but around everything I did with my life. I
learned that when we first begin our grieving, everything is very sticky, very messy. The situation looked

like an amorphous, overwhelming, intricate tangle of pain, something that would take me over. But with the help of a guide and friends I have learned to sort out the feelings that were mine from those that were given to me by someone else—my parents, or the culture, or whatever.

Previously, the pain had been just too great to bear, so I had cut it off and built a structure of denial around it. What therapy has shown me is that until that core is pierced the denial stays in place, since those memories are so strongly encoded in the body. The only way to release them is to grieve them, to re-experience them. Healing is more than just coping with the pain. Healing is more than just becoming functional and pleasant around other people; it's learning to feel again.

There were so many times during those years when I felt overwhelmed—by life, by feelings. But what I've come to learn is that being overwhelmed is from carrying more than your own share of grief and loss. Your personal loss can be coped with, but it's too much to expect one person to carry her own grief *plus* that of her parents, or any other family members who are still in denial. I no longer fear being swallowed by this huge pit of agony that I lived with for twenty-five years. I have separated my grief and my responsibility for my life from the pain of not being able to "save" my mother, who couldn't feel anything, and my father, who was schizophrenic.

We are not responsible for everything that was done to us as children. I gave up my child ultimately because I didn't feel capable of being a reasonable parent. I simply didn't have a role model for that. And that is something else to be grieved.

I'm very encouraged by my progress now. I wel-

come children coming to me. I've reowned the part of
me that has always been a mother.

It had been a long interview, and Mary was sitting
back in her chair now, breathing deeply and looking spent
but satisfied. She had given us so much to work with that
I ventured to ask her one more question. How might she
counsel another woman in a situation similar to her own?
What would she say to someone who was grieving the loss
of a child she had never really known? Mary answered
these questions with strength and conviction.

Realize that whatever decision you made is not a mark
against you; it's not indelible. I believed that my life was
over then. Only by unraveling my denial system, bit by
bit, did I grasp that it could be dealt with. So try to
honor whatever decision you made. No one can stand on
the outside and make a decision for someone else.

You also can't expect a change in attitude and
understanding to switch overnight. For me I had to
turn around twenty-five years of holding to the decision that it wasn't worth getting involved in relationships. I had a lot of momentum around my denial.
With denial, time is irrelevant. The wound is the
wound. It never goes away until you drop down into it
and try to heal it. Conscious awareness allows things
to grow and change. The more I did that, the more I
learned to face myself compassionately, to free myself
of the self-judgments and inner resentments around
the decision. That gave me honor and self-respect.

If you are thinking of trying to contact your son or
daughter again, you are at an advantage if you can do
that with a sense of inner balance. The more you
have accepted yourself, the easier it will be to meet
your child as a friend. And that can be a whole new
beginning, an awakening of a relationship. On the

other hand, for some people the meeting with this
new person who was your child may be very difficult
or unpleasant. It's important to feel strong enough in
yourself that you can carry whatever might present
itself. But that doesn't mean that you have to be a
one-hundred-percent "together person" before you
ever contact your child, just as you can't be one-hundred-percent knowledgeable about having children
before you ever have them.

You are still a mother or a father, face it. Just
because you don't have the child around is not necessarily the point. Many people aren't willing to look at that.
They stay in a safe prison of denial, being irresponsible
or immature. There is real power in just waking up
every morning and saying to yourself, "I have a child."

(See the Resource Guide at the end of this book for
the name of a national organization that helps connect
adoptees with birth parents as well as groups that give
counseling for decisions about adoption.)

SELF-CARE IN TIMES OF GRIEVING

Think of it this way: you are going to have to "mother"
yourself for a while as you grieve. And some of you won't
find that easy because you didn't have a nurturing mother
to begin with. Grief disorganizes your life, and that may
cause you to neglect the attention and routines that maintain your energy and health.

It's understandable. It takes an enormous amount of
effort to simply survive when you are grieving. In some
ways the major part of grieving is just surviving—surviving long enough for time to ease the intensity of the pain,

surviving long enough for the help you've been looking for to find you. That may leave very little energy left over for basic self-care, let alone for nurturance.

You may be feeling especially confused, or sad, or fearful, or just plain angry. As you mourn the loss of a child or a relationship with a child, you will be reliving some of your own childhood feelings as well as feelings you experienced at the time of your loss that didn't get adequately expressed. They may relate to yourself, such as thinking that you have made some terrible mistake, or they may concern your parents or family, or a system or institution, or a church, or God. But if you don't have a clear and appropriate way to release those feelings, you might end up by punishing yourself—through neglect or through indulgence. As we mourn any child-related loss we need to consider the child inside ourselves as needing special care.

Painful grieving drives many people back to their addictions. The temptation is always there to cover up sorrow with a familiar and convenient form of temporary relief. So we drink, or we smoke, or we eat. And sometimes it helps—for a short time. A glass of wine, or a sleeping pill, or a few extra sweets can have a place in assuaging a pain that feels too great to bear. But if these activities pass the level of moderation, we can easily set ourselves up for heavier consequences in the long run.

Grief weakens the immune system, suppressing the activity of our lymphocytes, the white blood cells that counteract bacteria and other infections. In a 1983 study at Mount Sinai School of Medicine, researchers found that men whose wives died of breast cancer showed a significant suppression of lymphocyte activity, and this effect continued for months afterward.[1]

---

[1] Blair Justice, *Who Gets Sick* (Los Angeles: Jeremy Tarcher, 1988), pp. 188-9.

When the body is already weakened by a serious loss, it is wise to do whatever we can to ease the stress further.

Self-care starts with honoring the fact that you will probably need more sleep or more ways to rest. The relief offered by climbing back under the covers is, for many, analogous to going back into a safe womb. "I found it helpful to make my room very dark and to pile all my quilts and blankets on the bed and then get under them," Gerry reported about a particularly grief-filled period of her life. "I'd tell myself that I was going away for a while, or that I was going to stay here until I felt strong enough to come out." Putting your life on hold for a few hours may be beneficial. Afternoon naps, or even a day or more in bed, may be ways to convince your body that you can take care of it and that it doesn't have to get seriously sick in order for you to notice.

Nourishing food will be a tremendously beneficial medicine at times like this. Foods that soothe as well as provide sustenance, like hot, hearty soups, are to be prized when we one is grieving. Observe your cravings. You may notice that they revolve around foods that you associate with your childhood, like hot chocolate milk, or mashed potatoes, or some other familiar favorite. Be compassionate in allowing yourself to occasionally use these foods for their emotional healing value. And at the same time keep your diet strengthened by a good vitamin-mineral supplement. You will find many powerful herbal formulas and teas that help soothe over-stressed nerves. (Consult the Bibliography for an excellent book on using herbs for healing.)

For clues in your own nurturance, keep thinking about the ways in which parents encourage children's health. The simple and obvious things, like fresh air and sunshine, for instance, are as necessary for adults. "Get out of the house and run around outside," mothers say as they ease their kids into snowsuits and mittens. Even in harsh weather it will serve us to get out, to walk around. Besides the fact that air and sun are genuinely healing forces for the physical body, your spirits will be lifted, too, when you get to see a bigger piece of the sky.

A mother will hold her child, communicating the healing of touch, of warmth, of the security of human contact. Your own need for touch during times of grieving may be accentuated, and you may be embarrassed by the need you feel. If you have no other person who can genuinely supply you with the nurturing touch you crave, you can supply it for yourself in a number of creative ways. More and more, adults are willing to admit that they find comfort in holding a large teddy bear or other stuffed animal. It may be worth a try. You can also set aside a time when you simply lie down on your bed, or sit in a rocking chair or on the couch, and cradle yourself in your own arms, as if you were hugging yourself. Repeating gentle, self-accepting phrases to your inner child can have powerful and healthy-generating consequences, phrases like: "I welcome you," "I'm not going to leave you," "You are doing the best you can." And don't forget the option of getting a therapeutic massage. This can be a life-saver when the hunger for touch and contact has you feeling alone, drained, and empty. (See Chapter 10 for additional suggestions for encouraging physical health.)

FOR JOURNALLING

1. About self-care: What would nurture you now? Make a list of ten things you like to do that provide you with a sense of well-being. Determine to do one each day for the next week.

2. About denial: It is often difficult, if not impossible, to perceive our own denial strategies. It is often much easier to perceive the denial systems of other

people and then to start to guess about our own.
Consider and write about this: In what ways do you
think your spouse or closest friend is "kidding"
himself or herself? In other words, are there
aspects of life and topics that he or she doesn't
want to know about or talk about? Does he or she
allow the expression of emotions like anger, fear,
sadness, confusion?

Consider and write about the ways in which your
mother is or was in denial about her pain or loss.
Think about the denial patterns of your father, your
children, your church or religious organization,
your employer or employers, and even our country
and our culture. Write as much as you care to
about any of these topics, and when you have finished read back over what you have written.
Reflect upon whether you are in denial in any of the
same ways that these other people or groups are.
Write about this, too.

3. At the conclusion of all your writing or thinking,
   summarize what you have learned by responding to
   the following incomplete sentence:
   As a result of doing these exercises I am aware. . . .

4

Am I Going Crazy, or What?

I miss them, Andy and Amy
The sunlight in their eyes
Their faces as they look up at me.
I miss their smiles,
And their little shoes.
I miss their clothes strewn around the house
And their toys
And their leftover breakfast covered with a plate
And slipped into the back of the refrigerator.
But most of all I miss their constant love
Their hugs
And knowing that they need me.

BOB T.

Bob WROTE THESE words as a part of his journalling about
the loss of his two children through a custody settlement.
They bespeak the sadness of a man redefining the meaning of
the word *father*. He mourns the absence of his children in the
thousands of little things they did or said. His body cries out
for their touch, remembering it more clearly now, perhaps,
than he did when they were with him. He weeps for himself,
wondering who he is now that they are gone. He feels
enraged. He feels fearful. He feels confused. And covering
everything, like a huge grey mist, is the sadness he feels.

Juanita feels the same sadness. For weeks after she
learned that she was pregnant, she held her baby in the arms
of her imagination. She loved the fact that people referred to
her as "expecting." The dream of pregnancy had been long
desired. But a miscarriage turned that dream into another
nightmare, and soon she felt herself being drawn down into a
whirlpool of depression and self-hatred. She fights a voice
within herself that says she is "cursed"; secretly, she fears
that she will never be a mother—at least, not in the way she
had planned. She rages at times: "It just isn't fair!"

Bob and Juanita are each experiencing grief—the normal response to loss. More than sadness, which is what most
people think of in describing this state, grief is not just one
emotion but a complex series of reactions that will color their
world and affect all aspects of their lives.

THE PORTRAIT OF GRIEF

Losing a child, or a relationship with a child, is a unique
brand of loss. But the ways in which these losses affect the
body/mind are common and predictable. When we are grieving, some of us suffer confusion, or depression, or frequent

bouts of illness, or the loss of appetite, or extreme sadness, or discomfort at the sight of a happy couple, a happy family, or a child about the age of the one we have lost.

We may find ourselves saying and doing things that we would normally never do—criticizing others, cursing, drinking, feeling hatred and anger toward God or other people. One woman described a feeling of wanting to leap out of her skin, desperately needing a friend but at the same time afraid to ask for help. Some of us weep at anything, others laugh at seemingly inappropriate times. Our marriages get shaky, our other children start acting out, and for the first time we think seriously about suicide.

Unfortunately, we fail to label what we are going through as "grief." Instead, many of us think we are going crazy. It often looks to us as if everyone else seems to be able to keep themselves together, or to have a happy life—everyone except us. So of course we think there must be something seriously wrong in our quadrant of the galaxy. It is painful. And it is hard.

For Janet, a thirty-four-year-old woman in my grief class, a series of losses left her feeling on the edge of insanity. She wrote about her situation and shared her writing with me.

> During a two-and-a-half-year period I lost a baby as the result of an abortion, a good job because of a subsequent pregnancy that was high-risk, my husband (who left me), and a relationship with my oldest daughter, who started a pattern of running away. Toward the end of that year, feeling crazy and totally separate from the rest of the world and as if I had committed some horrible crime, I had to endure a custody hearing. Three strangers sat in judgement on me, determining the fate of my two-year-old child. No one ever told me, not even the three strangers who were supposed to be professionals, that pain and my

feelings were indicators that I was going through
grieving.

No one questioned me about how many losses had
been going on in my life during that past year alone, to
say nothing of the losses of my childhood. No one said,
"Janet, what you are feeling and experiencing is very
human. You are grieving, and there is nothing 'wrong'
with you. What you have lost and your grief from
those losses will change you and your life. This is a
part of your humanness. Be gentle and patient with
yourself, and give yourself the privilege of experiencing your grief." Why didn't anyone say this to me?

When you grieve, it's because something has been
wrenched away. It's normal to hurt, even if that something
is "nothing more than a dream" or an expectation. It doesn't
matter; when our hopes and expectations are crushed, even
temporarily, we feel pain.

A loss rips the covers off an accumulation of pain—
sometimes, the pain of a lifetime. Realize that, for you,
strong and strange emotions are no longer going to be the
exception. It is normal to experience tears, anger, sadness,
and tremendous ambivalence, and to long for something—
anything—to take the pain away. It is also normal to feel
guilt, shame, and remorse, and to want desperately to go
back and do things differently. People who are grieving,
whether they call it grief or not, will go over the details of
their loss in an attempt to find a reason for it. "What did I do
wrong?" or "What would have happened if . . . ?" It is also
common to feel nothing, which can sometimes be even more
frightening.

Grief is frightening for you because many of the things
that you would previously have defined as "crazy" are suddenly your moment-to-moment experience. Who would
imagine that an adult man or woman would feel so unsettled

at the prospect of decision-making that he or she would start to weep in a supermarket? Yet that incident and other seemingly "crazy" behavior is common.

Grief will affect our job performance, our ability to enjoy our food and our friends, our health, our finances, our sense of meaning and purpose in life—literally, everything. And it is precisely for this reason that our grief can be transformational.

Grief is cumulative. That means that the grief that you are experiencing now through the loss of your child or a relationship with a child is not solely the result of present circumstances. All the losses you have ever gone through, and especially any childhood losses and previous child-related losses, will be "dredged up" as you go through this one. In some ways, this makes your current grief even harder. And at the same time each experience of grief offers us the chance to heal not only the current loss but aspects of all our previous losses.

Ruth, an older woman who told us the story of her life without children, connected with some painful memories as she spoke. "Right now I'm feeling a lot of sadness. It's about my own childhood," she said. "I'm feeling sadness for the way things were for me then. The confusion. The dishonesty. The constant feeling that I couldn't trust my own experiences or feelings." And, like so many others, that individual sadness led her into a more universal question. "I'm also feeling sadness for the way in which the world has turned out for so many children. Why isn't it possible to raise children without abuse? That hurts so much."

This book is ultimately about the transformational nature of grief. Our losses in relationship to children can be healed in such a way that they are not forgotten; instead, the energy now being expended in protecting the wounds is freed up for use in building the life we missed, the life we've always wanted, the life we deserve. That energy can be used to address the wounds of others, too.

BOB'S STORY

Bob's story of divorce and subsequent separation from his children demonstrates how easily life can spiral out of control and leave one feeling rootless and abandoned. Like so many of his "brothers," Bob questioned his identity as a man now that he was no longer a full-time father.

> When the relationship with my wife started to break up, it got to be maddening. I lived in a universe of extremes. Everything was either all or nothing. I kept resolving to be different, hoping against hope that this would turn things around, but it didn't. We separated. I moved out to a small apartment. She kept the kids and the house. When the emotional stuff about my separation from the kids started to bubble up inside me, I kept putting it away. I simply didn't know how to deal with it. I came from a big Italian family, and in that tradition the whole purpose of life is to be with family. Naturally, I couldn't face the fact that this separation from family was happening to me.
>
> It was also hard to think about having my kids be with a woman I didn't know. Who was this person I had married? Who was I? The little things, decisions she would make, everything was "big" now for me. It felt like the end of the world to me.
>
> After the separation I wanted urgently to move away so that I could be with my old friends, especially my brother, but I decided to stay on for one year so that I could be with the kids more regularly during this period of transition. I'm really glad I did. Periodically, then, I started to experience being overcome with waves of grief. Seeing a child on the street, seeing another couple walking together—any of these little signals were enough to trigger the wave. At times I could hardly breathe with the pain of it. Some of the

time I would just miss the proximity to the kids; at other times I mourned for the loss of my role of father. I realized that was not my life any more. That was so hard to take. I had to accept that being a father was not "the be-all and end-all" of my existence.

There were times during this period when I thought I could honestly go crazy and never come out of it. It was such a huge shock: realizing that I had nothing to stand on any more, realizing that the worst thing in the world had happened. I literally couldn't take it. I walked around for a long time simply filled with dread. "I can't do it," I said to myself on numerous occasions. But I had to. You get schizoid, because you are two crazy people in one body, and it's truly like being in some kind of hell world. I was communing with some very deep, formative forces. It became physically maddening at times, as if I wanted to peel off my skin and leave myself behind. But madness is a coward's way out, even though it was sure tempting.

I was drinking regularly and smoking a lot during this time. In so many painful moments it seemed as if there were only two alternatives: either face up to my life or have another cigarette. The first alternative was simply too much to bear at that stage. My addictions convinced me that I still had a body, but meanwhile, a part of me was slowly dying. I coped with the pain by becoming more of a workaholic, on one hand, and at the other extreme zoning out—watching endless hours of TV. I was doing whatever I could to numb myself. This manner of coping was necessary, and I really don't regret it. It got me through. Even though I was being psychologically violent to myself, it seemed to help me to survive.

A shock of this magnitude shakes up your whole world. It changes everything. I realized that I had not owned myself or taken responsibility for my own life. I wasn't a man. I was, in many ways, still a child myself, riding on the coattails of others.

So I got into therapy myself. The therapist had me address the issues related to my own mother, and I was able to see that my mother was trying to suffocate me by ignoring me. She was ignoring the individual by making endless rules. With this therapist I finally allowed myself to be nurtured in a way that my own mother had never nurtured me. That work was priceless. Within four months I had made remarkable progress and was starting to face my life again.

THE WORK OF GRIEVING

Freud called the process Bob describes "grief work." And the word "work" is definitely warranted. Wherever you may be in your own journey in relationship to your loss, you are probably aware of the effort it takes to handle that loss.

Grief is work because life is one piece. That means that every day I encounter things that remind me of my pain: things I read, things I see, things that people say unwittingly. Each time, I feel again a twinge or a stab of the initial pain. Each event provides me another opportunity to cry, to pray, to attempt to integrate my loss into the whole context of life. I know that things will never be the same as they were before this loss. I grow to accept the fact that I cannot reclaim those lost years. Gradually, over time, if I am willing to face my loss squarely, I even experience a resurgence of hope, a taste of that wise innocence.

Grieving takes time, more time than we think we have and definitely more time than we want to spend. Part of the grief-denying culture is the pervasive message that things can be "fixed," and fast. But when we suffer the loss of a child there is no such thing as instant relief. Nevertheless, the pressures all around us keep encouraging us to settle into business as usual. Some people offer us easy solutions, but what they are really doing is asking us to feel better so that we won't disturb their lives any more. They hurt with us and for us, and they don't like that.

Realize that the process of grief is cyclical, too. We may work at it for a period of months or even for a year, thinking we have a handle on our pain, only to find a new turn in the spiral, bringing with it a pain heightened exquisitely by old memories. So don't let anybody rush you. And don't let yourself be tyrannized by the suggestions that you can "do it the right way." There is only one way to grieve: your way. And that will usually entail a lot of tears as you fumble, bumble, and stumble along the path.

It is my strong conviction that we will never really be given more than we can handle, regardless of the way it may feel at the time. The body/mind has built-in protective mechanisms that will kick in to prevent overload. But we need to do our part by not trying to rush it, or taking on more than we feel ready for, or trying to be brave or a martyr. The amount of courage and strength required to go through this grieving into healing is awesome. That's why you need friends and a support system. And that's where this book can be helpful to you, too.

The hardest thing about some losses is that we don't know if we've lost or not. The ambivalence, confusion, conflicting data, false hopes, and constant fears—this is the agony that confronts us and makes our times of waiting a living hell.

Grief is full of such painful waiting: times in which there is no definite answer, one way or the other, about whether the worst has happened or not. We wait for test results. We wait for the phone call that says that it's all over. We wait for morning.

And while we wait we don't know how to act. Should
we be relieved and allow ourselves to celebrate, or start to
regroup our forces to get ourselves on the road to healing
again? Should we keep praying, hoping against hope that
the end is not at hand, even though we suspect, somewhere
deep within ourselves, that it is? Should we call the doctor
and demand an answer, regardless of the time of night or the
inconclusiveness of the data that has already been collected?

Ambivalence, and confusion, and waiting intensify our
grief in a hundred different ways.

Most decisions, I have learned, are made on the basis of
insufficient data, and even when the "facts" are all in, we
realize that it is imperfect humans who have gathered the
facts. Answers are almost always tinged with doubt.

My friend Susan confirmed the same outrage, the sense
of going crazy, and of deep sadness that others reported
about their child-related losses. Two miscarriages within a
year and a half propelled her into some deep inner work—
work that forced her to face many painful issues and to deal
with constant ambivalence and self-doubt. It was at Susan's
urging that this book was conceived.

SUSAN'S STORY

Susan's story testifies to the normality of strange and
strong emotions, and to the possibility of a sane, grounded,
and compassionate transformation through grief. She told me,

> The thought of having children was both highly roman-
> tic and also terrifying for me. One part of me did not
> want them or the responsibility for them, but another
> part longed to bear children. And frankly, this continual
> dichotomy angered me.
>
> Then, a few years ago, several of my closest friends
> had babies. At the time, my partner and I were also
> attempting to conceive. All of a sudden I realized

that, the older I got, the more likely it became that I would miss my chance to have a child. It shocked me to discover that I was feeling competitive with my friends. I began to become increasingly tense about not becoming pregnant.

It surprised me even more that the predominant mood I felt about it all was shame. When I didn't become pregnant, I felt ashamed of myself. And despite my knowledge of psychology and years of self-observation that had formed a basis of my spiritual work, I was telling myself that I was, therefore, incomplete as a woman. Often I even spoke to my partner in the mood and posture of practically asking for forgiveness for not becoming immediately pregnant. And when I saw what I was doing, I was horrified. My action exemplified the whole patriarchal attitude I had worked so hard to eradicate from myself.

As time went on, accepting encouraging words became more and more difficult for me, and comments like "Relax," which my friends and mate were offering me, made things worse. Emotionally, I had worked myself up into a battle, willfully trying to force something that was completely out of my hands. And so I waited, in anguish, while my mate and I tried without success month after month after month. Nothing consoled me. In contrast to my fighting and bitterness, his silent strength and natural acceptance actually made things more unbearable.

I knew that I was up against the assumption that somehow a child was an answer, or that getting pregnant was some kind of prize that would prove my worthiness. And it was this attitude that I found the most distressing, since I had seen it in other women and knew it was false hope. I had observed that a child didn't fill that feeling of an "empty space" in a woman's being but often actually aggravated it.

Finally, the test was positive. I was pregnant. And that's when the real work began. I started remembering the reasons I was ambivalent about having children in the first place.

I remembered an inner vow that I had made as a very young child, a vow to never have children. Having been sexually abused by my father, I had, as my reference point for childhood, a bitter death of innocence. I had decided back then that there was no joy in bringing wonderful children into a life that offered only pains. Evidently, I still had a lot of grieving to do, and I was only beginning to see the extent of it.

Once I was able to take responsibility for that early decision and respect it for what it was—that is, the desperation of a child — I was able to approach releasing myself from it. But dealing with that wound only made me more sensitive to another one that lay beside it.

The fact of being pregnant now awakened fears and grave doubts about my capacity for mothering. I became distraught by observing how often I acted the way my parents did. All the things that I had resisted about them—the strict discipline and lack of affection in my father, for instance—were there in me, in seed form, and I could cite many examples in which they had shown themselves full-blown. And the more I felt these things, the more ashamed and confused I became. Was I the only unfit mother who had ever lived? How could something as natural as being pregnant, something that happens all the time to people all over the world, be so shattering to me?

Being pregnant did not do what I expected it to do! I needed to tell the truth about that before I could grieve it. I felt cheated, and that aroused anger at the way society exploits these phenomena—as if having a child will be the answer to misery and unhappiness and feelings of lacking wholeness. I did feel profound awe and joy at being able to conceive a being in my womb, yet part of me still remained cynical and unbelieving.

As a young child I was the victim of incest by my father. That ongoing experience of my early childhood had left traces of a belief that I was cursed, or at least forsaken by God. As a five-year-old I had asked, "How could God let something like this happen to me?" Now, as an adult and preparing to birth my own child, I experienced unresolved bitterness around the abuse, which began to poison the inherent joy and appreciation of the miracle of conception. I observed myself swinging from a mood of romanticism around having a child to one of cynicism, and in the course of my daily life I noticed fleeting thoughts about death and miscarriage, and I caught these words around me more frequently. It was a predictable phenomena, given my past experience: now that I had achieved this prize, I was convinced that something or someone was going to take it away. It was my mate who helped me to see that I was resisting a natural and joyful acceptance as a way of defending against the pain of future loss. Hadn't I counseled others in the same way? "We do it all the time," I remembered saying to a close friend in a similar situation. "We're afraid to feel our joy because we're afraid to feel our pain."

That encouragement lasted for a few days. I was high—glorying in taking, without question, whatever extra food or rest my body was asking for. I had even almost forgotten my fear that anything could go wrong until one day, after urinating, I saw some blood. In that moment I plunged right into the fear that I had been so happy to watch subside. I panicked.

"Don't worry," said one woman, "I spotted all through my first pregnancy." Another remarked, "I know a woman who bled heavily and now she has a seventeen-year-old son." These assurances provided some relief, though short-lived. Inside, and growing louder, was this nasty voice that would say, "I knew it. I knew something was going to go wrong. You don't deserve to have good things happen."

The midwife was great. She exuded a "no-problem" attitude as she cautioned me that we would just take things a day at a time. We had figured I was eight or ten weeks pregnant at this point, yet she had been unable to pick up a heartbeat. Still, she assured me, this was not necessarily a bad sign. So, buoyed up, once again I went home with plans to take it easy.

Then one evening I awoke in the middle of the night and went to the bathroom. That's when I saw it. Something besides blood had been released from my body. An undefinable piece of matter. I knew that I was losing the fetus.

It was like a bad dream. My body began cramping violently, and in my delirium and tears I remember crying out loud to the child, "I thought you were a March baby. I thought you were a March baby," repeating this phrase over and over, inconsolably, like a crazy woman. In this moment I realized how much I had truly wanted to have this child. The love for this being overwhelmed me, and as I swooned in my tears I was everymother wailing for her lost child.

My feelings were so bizarre—profound grief coupled with an overwhelming love and appreciation for life; awesome attachment and caring for someone I had never physically met, touched, talked to. I experienced the grief and sorrow as waves. They would come and grip me completely, squeezing me like a sponge. And then they would go, and there would be a void. It was like being moved by something bigger than I was, and with that came a strange freedom and peace. I've learned for myself and in talking to others that this peace follows upon surrender to the inevitable. Relief. After weeks of spotting and not knowing whether this pregnancy was a "go" or not, it was so good just to know.

The next morning, however, all the cosmic acceptance and sweetness that had graced me the night before were gone. I tasted only the bitterness. It was the emotional roller-coaster ride all over again.

The ultrasound procedure confirmed what I knew. My body had produced all the equipment to nurture and care for a fetus, but, the physician told me, it was possible that no being had actually nested in my womb, or that if one had, he or she was not destined at this time to stay.

Another plunge. Humiliation. Anger. To think that there had being nothing there was beyond my comprehension. I was convinced that I had felt the presence of a being who wanted to take birth through me. "Is there no end to this painful ride?" I cried softly. Yet, in hearing the physician's words, again I felt relieved of a burden. Nothing is scarier than the unknown.

With the help of my friends and midwife I finally explained to myself that the being had entered my aura, but had not yet taken human form. Of course, no tests will ever confirm that. But it was important for me to have that sense of closure about the why of things.

It took a full seven months, since I chose not to have a "D and C" (dilation and curettage, the common hospital procedure for removing unnecessary tissue

from the uterus), for my body to begin to feel ordinary and more relaxed hormonally. And throughout
this time my grief continued. "What nobody warned
me about were the mood swings," my friend Judith
told me in sharing her own experience of miscarriage.
"As if the sadness of losing the child were not enough,
I had the extra pain of trying to carry on business as
usual while the hormones were running rampant
throughout my body." I laughed along with her,
although the memories weren't pleasant ones. "It's a
miracle my husband and friends didn't give up on me,"
she confided as if she really believed they would. "I
was all over the place."

I called the midwife periodically for consolation or
just to chat. What a wise woman she was, too. She
warned me that other people were not going to understand what I was going through. "It is natural to feel
hurt, annoyed, or even angered by their suggestions,"
she cautioned. How many times had I heard them
already: "Oh, you'll get pregnant again," they said,
meaning well but missing the point. Another woman,
who thought she was being empathic, said, "I don't
know what to say," and I immediately felt as if I were
supposed to be comforting her. When you're hurting
that much, the last thing you need is to have to carry
your supposed supporters, too.

The midwife, herself having had one miscarriage
and five children, shared with me her feeling that no
other pregnancy had ever made up for the loss of her
miscarried child. To this day she still wakes up in the
middle of the night with nightmares and tears just
around the time of year that this baby's birth was due.

She encouraged me not to underestimate the pro-
fundity of the grief I felt, despite the short duration of
my pregnancy. And although many women who mis-

carry as early do not bond with the being so strongly
as I did, others do. The depth of that bond is one factor that determines the depth of one's grief and the
subsequent length of time it will take to heal.

The midwife also confirmed the normal reaction of
fear I was beginning to sense at the thought of getting pregnant again. "Because you have no other children, your only reference to the process of pregnancy
is one of loss," she advised. "The only way that will
change," she assured me warmly, "is carrying a child
full term. That alone will give you a new point of reference."

Four months later my partner and I began to try
again, and almost immediately the round of confusion
was upon us. My menstrual cycle was highly irregu-
lar—at one point, forty-two days—my hormones were
crazy, and I was experiencing nausea. Was I pregnant? Was my upset emotional state due to the flux of
residual pregnancy hormones? Was it all just my
intense desire to be pregnant that had me creating
my symptoms psychologically? More shame. More
embarrassment at the thought that I might be making
it all up. More tests with positive results. Yet a few
days later I was bleeding and cramping.

Breakdown. This not-knowing fed my already
strong feelings of deficiency. I began to feel crazy
again. The thought of having to go through this experience repeatedly was horrific.

This time the ultrasound procedure indicated that
all my symptoms were most likely due to the earlier
pregnancy. My body was evidently still producing
enough hormones to create a reading of pregnancy.
Just another piece of objective data, but for me it was
another last straw in a seemingly endless progression.
I was enraged. Anger colored everything in my world,

an experience that I have heard described as "being
plunged into the underworld." My bitterness and
resentment grew stronger and more visible, and my
friends noticed. It became intolerable for me to be
around them and their children; I couldn't bear to listen to them talk about diapers and nursing. Every time
I did errands in town I saw at least one pregnant
woman, or I'd run into a beautiful little toddler who
would walk up to me and say hello. Inside, I was full of
fury, waging my personal battle with God who, I was
convinced, was rubbing my nose in the fact of this pain.

The anger stripped away more of my defenses
against the memories of the sexual abuse. I recalled
that when my mother was pregnant with my younger
brother, my father increased the abuse of both my sister and me. One night, whimpering and sobbing in my
pillow, terrified that I was going to get pregnant by my
father, I said something to him. His response was so
angry and ridiculing that I somehow gathered that
childbearing was for good people and sex was for bad
people. Those assumptions took root deep inside me.

Years later, as a teenager, I was tough and rebel-
lious. Sex and drugs and rock music provided a way
out. "No way am I going to have kids," I boasted. "I
don't want to deal with any brats running around me."
After all, I was for sex, not for childbearing.

As I grieved these startling memories, my mate
and loved ones kept encouraging me to face all the
emotions, feelings, and thoughts, as many as I was
capable of facing, rather than try to escape them.
This was grief work! Wrenching. Devastating at
times. Lonely. But it paid off. A year later, and pregnant again, I could definitely see the growth that had
taken place for me. I felt so grateful that I had not
birthed a child without having gotten in touch with

the pain and the feelings of my inner child. Even when, seven weeks into the pregnancy, the spotting started again, I found that, unlike the way I reacted during the first miscarriage, I didn't respond with such archaic terror to the sight of the blood. I felt a greater trust of the body's natural processes, and I actually allowed myself to relax—for the time being.

One evening, however, with a large gathering of friends at the house, I left the meeting and went to the bathroom. The spotting had increased. Without warning I began to sense the onset of a possible psychotic episode. I felt as if I were on the edge of a cliff and that I wasn't going to be able to handle the situation that I sensed was starting. I called one of my women friends, who joined me almost immediately, and began to tell her all my fears. She just sat there with me, holding my hand. "I can't do this again," I sobbed, shaking my head back and forth as I began to spiral down. My friend, who is also a therapist, just cut right to the bone. "Stop it," she said, looking me full in the face. "You don't need to do this," and her firmness was so full of love that when I looked in her eyes I knew that I had a choice not to go crazy. "Stay here," she said firmly, meaning "Stay present to what is going on; don't let yourself opt for craziness."

I can't tell you how helpful it is to be with someone who is not trying to cheer you up but is just there listening. With her solid support I was able to draw strength from within myself, strength that I didn't know I had.

Having other women around at a time like this is extremely important. No one should have to go through these things alone.

That night I dreamed that a confident male physician had announced to me, "Everything is going to be fine."

The ultrasound was immediately conclusive: it

showed the same condition as before. Only this time
we knew why. Without medical support I would be
unable to carry a pregnancy to full term because my
body wasn't producing hormones in sufficient quanti-
ty. My doctor assured me that, knowing this, we
could remedy the problem, and he spoke the words
exactly as I had heard them in my dream the night
before: "Everything is going to be fine."

On the ride home that day I expressed to my
female companion how loved I was feeling. Both
these miscarriages had unearthed many of my
undealt-with psychological issues, and I was grateful
to be able to address these issues without a child in
my arms. I knew then that when I did become pregnant the timing would be perfect, and that recognition
filled me with a sense of trust that was the opposite to
the feeling of being cursed. I knew then that my history of abuse was no longer my obstacle to God but my
doorway. It was a section of the labyrinth I had been
given to work with in this life.

Turning to my friend, I said confidently,
"Remember when I looked at you and said, "I don't
want to have to go through that again"? Well, I don't.
I'm evolving with this. My mourning and grieving
don't have to be predicated on a lack of self-worth. I
feel worthy just because I'm alive, and I feel that life
is truly a magnificent thing."

A few days later I was on an airplane. We hit some
turbulence, and without a second thought I put my
hands on my belly, as I had done so many times
before, and explained to the baby that it was just
bumpy air. Then I remembered that I had miscarried,
and the tears began to flow. I wept softly but deeply,
missing this little ritual that had formed between me
and this baby. My mate, noticing my upset, looked at

me with concern. "What's wrong?" he asked gently. I explained that it was already such a natural habit for me to talk to the baby that I forgot that the baby was gone. He understood, and I noticed that his eyes, too, were moist. "That's a wonderful habit to have," he said, and I cried some more. Without resistance and bitter self-hatred, I felt the grief wash over me, and the depth to which I could feel it became food for my soul.

COMMON FEARS/COMMON QUESTIONS

Despite the vast differences in each type of loss in relationship to children, some factors in the experience of the loss, or in the mourning of the loss, are reported commonly. It may help you to feel less alienated, less "crazy," in knowing that others have lived through, and even healed through, feelings or stages similar to yours.

I invite you to slowly read over the list that follows and to note which of these common experiences may have troubled you. As you grow to accept these feelings, thoughts, or questions as normal, you give yourself another brick with which to build a strong foundation for your healing.

Common Fears:

- to fear you are cursed, or even evil; to fear that everything you touch or everything you try to do will result in some sort of failure or catastrophe.
- to fear an empty future, old age, dependence, and financial ruin.
- to fear death more acutely, coupled with a secret hope that you might die so that your pain would be over.
- to fear that this sense of being out of control, or emotionally devastated, is never going to end.

Common Experiences:

- to wake up in panic, worrying about things that

never bothered you before; to want to run away—
to leave the place in which this pain took place so
that you don't have to be reminded of it.

- to make bargains with God, or with yourself, hoping
  against hope that something will change your circumstances magically.
- to try out some new "approach" every day, looking
  for a therapy, a technique, a "cure."
- to find yourself wandering around the house, or
  staring out the window, wondering what to do next.
- to like the specialness, the caring, the attention you
  may get from others, and to feel guilty about that.
- to wish that you could pray, or be more patient, and
  not be able to.
- to "rerun" all the low points in your life, and to feel
  again the pain of all your previous losses.
- to long for your own mother or father, even if he or
  she was or is emotionally unavailable to you.
- to be so overwhelmed by having to make one more
  decision that you may break down and start to cry
  when asked what you want for lunch.
- to dread "family" gatherings.
- to "see" your child in a crowd, or "hear" your child's
  voice, or dream vividly about holding and nursing
  your child, even if you have not had a child.
- to experience deep remorse for all the ways in
  which you have hurt others.
- to see and hear nothing but pain and tragedy in the
  world around you, and to actually feel the pain of all
  the men or women who are going through a situation similar to yours.
- to start having flashbacks of aspects of your childhood, particularly the times of fear, deprivation, or
  abuse.
- to search around for something to fill in the void

created by this pain, and to find it in addictive behavior.

- to be more accident-prone, or more susceptible to illness.
- to discover that all your relationships are strained, even with those whose help you need or want the most.

Common Feelings:

- to fear that you are losing touch with reality.
- to feel helpless in the face of something you can't fix.
- to plague yourself by wondering if you've ever "done enough."
- to feel guilty because you are secretly relieved when you finally find out the facts of your case.
- to feel embarrassed around others whenever the subject of children comes up.
- to resent anyone who seems to have a happy life, especially anyone who has a child.
- to feel some anger or resentment toward the child, or children, whom you have lost.
- to feel embarrassed and not want to share your story, let alone your feelings, with other people, for fear that they will not understand—or, worse, that they will condemn you.
- to feel so depressed that you don't have the energy to change your clothes or brush you teeth.

Common Questions:

- "Why?" or "How did this happen to me?" or "Where did I go wrong?"
- "Am I a complete woman?" "Am I a real man?"
- "Where is God in all this?"

Sometimes, professional help will be useful and even necessary in dealing with these issues, but it still doesn't mean that your responses aren't common and normal. (For more about when professional help is needed, see Chapter 10.) At this point it is important to give yourself the permission to feel your pain, and the assurance that, like most of us, you too will survive. You will.

FOR JOURNALLING

The suggestions that follow are designed to help you bring your hidden fears and questions to light. Writing about your feelings will give you more clarity about them, and contacting your own inner wisdom will help you feel more balanced and sane.

1. Letter to a Friend. Look over the lists above and check off any items that you currently identify with. Use your journal to write about one (or more) most troubling to you now. You might imagine that you are speaking about this feeling or experience to a trusted friend. Use the form of a letter, or just write freely about it.

2. Remembering Your Resources. It often happens that we carry around many questions that could be answered by people who know: physicians, financial advisers, other men or women who have had similar experiences. First, make a list of some of your questions or the confusing elements of your situation; list things you are ambivalent about or some of the unpredictable factors connected with your loss. Go back over the list and note each item with a name or resource that could supply some information or help. Decide to get some of that help as soon as possible.

3. Inner Wisdom Speaks. Admittedly, some of your questions and concerns can be answered only by yourself. One of many ways to access your inner

wisdom is to try writing about your concerns from a different perspective: for instance, imagine yourself five years from now, looking back on this current period of your life. Imagine that you are "whole," healthy, happy. Describe in as much detail as possible how you achieved this.

4. Conclusion. Read over what you have written. Now complete the following statement: As a result of writing or thinking about these considerations I am aware. . . .

5

No One
to Blame
but Myself

*"What kind of a person gives her
child away?" the shaming voice
asked, the lips curling around the
words as if they smelled bad.
Granted, it was only a dream, but
not too far from the reality I was
experiencing all around me, day
after day.*

HELEN G.

THE WOMAN who shared her dream with us was nearly
fifty, and the dream had happened more than twenty-five
years earlier. But she recalled the details of it as if it had
happened the previous week. Over the years I have considered with many others the enormous guilt and shame often

connected with any type of loss of a child, infertility, or the decision to be child-free.

It is amazing how much guilt and shame are attached to losing—as if it were some sort of cardinal sin. When we lose someone or something dear to us, when we lose a dream or an expectation, when we lose a relationship to a part of ourselves, or even when we lose something that we didn't want anyway, we commonly feel guilt. We replay in our minds a thousand details connected with the loss, and with each detail we ask: "Did I do enough?" or "Did I do too much?" or "Did I do the wrong thing?" Especially in the initial stages of our mourning, the answers to these questions will generally not be weighted in our favor.

Despite the tremendous input of popularized psychology and self-help programs, my experience is that vast numbers of us, in the western cultures at least, tend to view ourselves quite harshly. We operate from a deeply-rooted sense of unworthiness—undoubtedly the result of the way in which we were treated harshly as children or influenced strongly by a religious upbringing based on fear of a punishing God. We may not show this when we're busy, when we are accomplishing, or when things are going in our favor, but when our walls of defense are attacked by grief and pain, these insecurities start to color our perceptions. We fear that when the last vote is in we will be found lacking, and we will stand exposed, all our darkest secrets revealed. We don't accept that our darkness is part of the wholeness of who and what we are. We are ashamed of what others will feel or say about us. We are ashamed of ourselves. We are guilty that we didn't meet our own or others' expectations.

In times of stress, as when we have lost something, we commonly increase the stress by flagellating ourselves with the recollections of "if only I . . ." despite our knowledge that hindsight is always a luxury.

A touching scene in the film *Paradise* portrays a confrontation between a husband and wife who have for many months been agonizingly distant from each other. Their dialogue reveals to us their increasing estrangement over the death, three years ago, of their child. The baby had accidentally choked to death in his crib while his mother was in another room. In this gripping scene, when the husband's frustration at his wife's coldness has reached a breaking point, he grabs her violently. Provoked beyond her defenses and now wracked with tears, the woman confesses to her husband, at long last, that she had heard the child's cry that afternoon—a familiar cry, like the one she had heard every day. She sobs the bottled-up pain of years when she admits that she heard the silence following the cry and had assumed that the baby had simply gone back to sleep. At last she is speaking, out loud, her guilt and regret that perhaps she could have saved him if only she had gone to him in that moment. If only she hadn't waited.

It is a scene that is repeated, with greater or lesser intensity, in almost every situation of loss. The woman who loses a pregnancy through miscarriage or gives birth to a handicapped child asks, "What did I do wrong?" The parent who loses custody of his or her child through a bitter divorce mourns with great anguish what might have been. The woman who decides to give up her child for adoption or the one who decides not to have children may, even if she feels basically at peace with her choice, still have moments of wondering about her decision, or bodily sensations of longing when she sees another mother attending a child. "If only I . . . ," she may lament in times of depression or stress. And it may be exceedingly challenging to fight the voices of condemnation that still rise up within herself, voices that she has internalized from harsh parents or from a demanding and uncompassionate culture.

In times when people most need the support and acceptance of others, they often find themselves alone. Maybe because they "just don't know what to say," or because the recognition of another's loss is a trigger for their own, other people will exclude you from their lives now that you are grieving. And that can intensify your fears and feelings that you are "bad" or have "done something wrong." They don't necessarily mean to give you that message, but when you're hurting, that's frequently the way you'll interpret it.

Grief looks for a scapegoat, for someone to blame, for someplace to lay the burden of this outrage, this confusion, this fear. When there is no one "out there" to thrust it upon, it is normal for us to internalize the blame, taking on responsibility for things that were actually out of our control.

Even many years after the fact, men and women need to tell their stories and verbalize the guilt, the secret fears they have been harboring. Even if they know now, intellectually, that their guilt is unrealistic, that they couldn't be every place at once, that they couldn't give what they didn't have, that they couldn't guard against every eventuality, they may need to hear these reminders anyway—many times, in fact—from the lips of a caring friend or witness, in order for the demon to be exorcised for good, or at least until the next time of extreme vulnerability. Some wounds never heal. But, with the support of others, we all learn to live with our pain. Some of us even become the more compassionate for it.

GUILT AND SEX, AND THE LOSS OF CHILDREN

Children come through the act of sex. They come from our naked bodies, from between our legs. They come naked, too, covered with blood and fluids. They come, if they do, therefore, inextricably bound to our beliefs, our fears, and the accumulated guilt and pain associated with the fact that we

are incarnate—that is, in the flesh. A midwife-friend reported that during labor, women will commonly reveal their atti-
tudes about their bodies and sexuality. A woman who has
been sexually abused, for instance, will sometimes stop her
labor, postponing her dilation beyond a certain point. "It is
as if to say," the midwife told me, "that place 'down there' is
scary, or dirty, or not to be acknowledged. And I don't want
my baby coming through there."

As a teenager, Robin was distraught that her body
wasn't developing, that she hadn't started menstruating
when all her friends already had their periods for several
years. Yet, despite Robin's repeated requests for help and
answers, her mother refused to deal with the situation. "My
shame grew day by day," reported Robin. "I felt completely
isolated in my pain and confusion. I think the shame she felt
for her own body, and the fact that she was probably abused
as a child, kept her from wanting anything to do with taking
care of mine."

For Renee, a forty-year-old mother of three children,
who had two abortions in her early twenties, her guilt didn't
show up until the age of thirty-five when she failed to
become pregnant at the time that she wanted to. "I wondered if it might be a punishment for having had two abortions," she admitted, "even though I don't believe that God
works that way. Still, I was tempted to feel frightened about
it." Today she is clear about her early decisions but admits
that she is surprised how much guilt is still a part of her
response under stress.

For Laura, a single woman in her fifties, the resolution
of her guilt around an abortion was more challenging. "I
carry around a lot of guilt for what I did, even though I've
worked it all out in therapy, and I feel alright with God. But I
never got married, and I never had children, and I miss that."

Despite the almost pornographic obsession of the media
with sex, we still live in a society that has numerous taboos

against the relaxed innocence of the body. We are bound, therefore, to have our negative self-judgments reinforced by others
when sex results in the conception of children outside marriage, or when we choose an abortion, or when we can't conceive, and even when we adopt or choose to remain child-free.

Dana, a well-educated woman who had recently given
birth after several miscarriages and years of working with
infertility, reported that as a teenager her mother instilled in
her a tremendous fear of unwanted pregnancy by telling her
over and over, "Don't get pregnant. Just make sure you don't
get pregnant."

Our guilt—or, more specifically, shame—in regard to
sex is taught us, either directly or by implication. No child
comes into the world with that shame. In fact, the situation is
exactly the opposite. Children exhibit unbounded sexuality
in the form of free-flowing life energy. They display no inhi-
bitions until these are imposed. Nevertheless, once learned,
this guilt and shame has profound implications for the way
we live our lives, the choices we make in regard to children,
and the health of our bodies.

A PIECE OF MY STORY

Confusion, fear, and guilt around sexuality catalyzed my own
inability to bear children. This is the way it built in me:

> At twenty-eight, eight months after my marriage, I
> had a total hysterectomy, which was supposedly nec-
> essary medically. I am convinced that my condition
> was the result of long-held guilt and the repression of
> sexuality. In fact, I know it.
>
> I was an impressionable Catholic child. And
> although I received little education about sex, what I

did get from the Church had to do mostly with sin. In preparing for confession we were told that it was a sin to touch yourself, and at first I wasn't sure what that meant—did it mean you couldn't touch your hand, or your shoulder, or what? I realized slowly that you don't touch yourself "down there." That was the place that was "disgusting." It was as if I had a live bomb in my body—something that could blow up at any time and send me to Hell. Out of fear, then, I became obsessed with trying not to commit sin. I wanted only to do the right thing so that God would not condemn me.

Catholic kids weren't supposed to talk about sex or act "immodest" in any way. I had four sisters, all within a few years of my age, and yet we never even dressed in front of one another. I even locked the bathroom door to change into my pajamas—all private and secret. I don't remember ever seeing my parents naked.

The fear of the body was deeply ingrained by the time I was a teenager. In the early years of high school I began to put two and two together about sex. But even then I was so naive about the mechanism of sexuality that I always imagined that a woman's belly opened up to give birth. I never knew the baby came out between her legs.

At camp one summer I heard the girls talking about a teenager who had a baby, and I asked, "Was she married?" And they said: "No!" And I couldn't understand that. As far as I was concerned, God sent you babies only when you were married.

Sex was terrifying because I believed, as a result of the kind of religious instruction I got, that just to think about it was a sin; then I'd have to go to confession. Otherwise there was this tremendous battle going on inside me. I would think about sex to try and

figure it out, and yet when I thought of it I'd have to
confess that I had committed sin.

For a couple of years I actually became obsessive
with trying to rid myself of the guilt connected with
these "sins." I'd wash my hands forty or fifty times a
day. This was at age fourteen, so naturally my mother
was concerned about me. She did send me on a
retreat led by some nuns, hoping I would get some
special help there, but I don't remember that it did
any good, except that I liked the fact that my mother
was concerned about me. That was important.

Even after the obsessions stopped I felt fear
around sexuality. When I did spend time with boys it
always involved friendship-type activities—never any
threatening encounters.

From the time I was a young child I had a strong
desire for God and service and a tremendous will to do
the best thing, the "good" thing. As I understood it
then, in the Catholic tradition it was holier to be a nun
than a mother, and since I always desired the "high-
est" calling I went into the convent at age eighteen.

I adored being a nun. The life of silence and prayer
introduced me into domains of the heart that were profound and richly satisfying, and I would leap out of bed
in the morning, ecstatic to greet the day. For years and
years I was carried along on a wave of bliss. It was all I
ever wanted.

But I know my body suffered. My menstrual periods were excessively heavy, and I always had very
painful cramps and headaches. I was also occasionally
thrown back into the obsessive scruples of my early
adolescence, and I talked to many of my confessors
about it, although without coming away with a sense
that they understood what was happening.

My body must have been quite constricted, too. I

remember some of the other nuns talked about using tampons, so I tried one, too, but could not get it to go in. I didn't even know my body well enough to find my vagina. My friend Sister Stephanie, whose father was a physician, tried to help me, but we couldn't do it. There were other physical cues, too, now that I think about it.

I left the convent in 1971, after eight full years. I didn't leave to get married but rather to follow another calling, knowing that the Holy Spirit had other plans for me. The nuns wept when I left. I never looked back.

In 1973, eight months after my marriage, I went to a clinic for a routine pap smear. The physician felt something large and didn't know what it was. Was it cancer? So a few days later I went into the hospital for tests, followed by surgery.

I gave my permission to do what was necessary, and when I woke up I learned that the surgeon had done a total hysterectomy—ovaries, uterus, cervix—and had even taken out my appendix for good measure. Initially, I was relieved that I didn't have cancer. It was "only" endometriosis, a condition that had supposedly destroyed the ovaries.

At the time, the loss of the ability to have children did not seem that crucial. But, no one really invited me to grieve my loss, either. I think everybody was just relieved that I seemed to be taking it so well. The fact of childlessness was simply not mentioned—by anyone.

Before the operation I remember calling my parents, who lived across the country, and telling them not to bother making a trip to be with me. I'm sure I was protecting them, but I was also protecting myself, since I certainly didn't want to have to be any braver than I was already being.

I know I was very frightened at the time, but the fears, instead of being expressed directly, came out in the form of being absolutely compliant about my doctor's decision and to the hospital routine. "If I'm good," I'm sure I was thinking, "then God won't punish me." That was the theme of my life then, and something that I work with all the time now.

I feel fairly confident that if that operation hadn't happened I would have had children. I'm not sure I had a tremendous desire to have them, but I'm sure I would have, just because it was the "right thing"—the expected thing—to do.

That was almost twenty years ago. Since then, on rare occasions, I've felt a strong desire to bring a child into my life and share the experience with my husband. I've never felt that he was opposed to the idea, but I never felt he was excited about it, either. So, whenever that desire arose, I would consider adopting a child, but in a few weeks or months my enthusiasm for the idea would fade. It was more a fantasy of what would enliven our married relationship, I think, or something I could show my parents to prove that I'd done right.

Perhaps we missed a big opportunity in never adopting a child. I think about that often. Perhaps that would have given me a deeper sense of compassion, a greater opportunity to learn selfless service, which is what I've always wanted in my life. I have to make my peace with these considerations every time they come up.

It is shocking to see how much anguish I've put myself through in my life—anguish that all stemmed from a need to prove my worth to a punishing, righteous, demanding God. I've paid a high price for that. I lost my ovaries, my uterus, and my cervix to that God!

And I was brave about it, too. "Hey, if that's the
price of purity, or goodness, here, take it. . . ." What a
sad thing! I was guilt-ridden for years. I've played
out being celibate, denying my body, while at the
same time being wildly unconventional, both in the
convent and afterwards in an attempt to break out of
the tyranny of repression. But it was a nightmare.
Really it was, when I let myself admit it.

HEALING GUILT

Feelings of guilt may always hang around me. They are
strongly ingrained. But I have learned to live with them,
recognize them for what they are, and many times simply
refuse to be run by them. Probably the biggest help in dealing with guilt or shame is to begin to honor the body. For
me, that started with learning some body disciplines that
approach the body with compassionate attention: through
some relaxation processes, through Yoga, through dance and
massage. Certainly these are not the whole story, but they
can be a valuable beginning. The body will hold the memories of pain in particular organs and cells. Years later, when
those parts are worked with through forms of therapeutic
touch, these memories and the specific feelings associated
with them can be released.

Writing this book, and listening to the stories of others'
shame and guilt around the body and around the loss of children, has been a profound healing for me.

Telling my own story was another way to clear away
unrealistic guilt and shame. It has again allowed me to lay
responsibility where it belongs and to relinquish it from
where it doesn't.

Being without children has been a blessing in many

ways. It has led my husband and me to live together with other people, including children, and to finally settle into the spiritual community in which we reside today. We now participate in the lives of many children, some of whom we live with.

I have lost something, and I will mourn that. I hope I will mourn more and more as the years go by, not because I want to wallow in pain but because such mourning keeps my heart open so that I may be available to know and witness to the pain of others. My grief is a foundation upon which to build something else. Something eternal.

Yoga Journal once carried an empowering story about a group of American Buddhist women who held a ceremony of remembrance and acceptance about their choices regarding children.

Japanese Buddhists have a deity named Jizo, who protects travelers, including those who are journeying into and out of life. It is said that Jizo also takes care of the souls of miscarried and aborted babies. The statue of Jizo depicts a monk with a baby face, sometimes holding a jewel in his hands. Traditionally, Japanese women sew bright red bibs for the Jizo figures, each bib commemorating the loss of one child.

In the contemporary ceremony described in this article, a group of forty women, ranging in age from twenty to seventy, sat together quietly sewing their red bibs while each woman told the story of her loss, her pain, her guilt about a miscarriage, an abortion, a child's death, or giving her child up for adoption.

"As we speak," wrote author Melody Ermachild, "the room fills with the presence of the beings who came to be with us, entered into our very bodies, and then left us again. Also with us are the many children and grandchildren we have borne, whom we are raising every day. In this ceremony our outer personas have dissolved in the grief we share as mothers. And this we share with all women in the world whose every pregnancy has not produced a healthy child raised to adulthood."

With the completion of the bibs the women approached the statue, one by one, and lay their symbolic offerings on its shoulders. They sprinkled some incense onto the burner at the statue's feet and then bowed in a gesture of humble respect before rejoining the circle of their companions.

Ermachild continues: "Together, we women have remembered our children, acknowledged their deaths, and bid them goodbye with wishes for their safety. Our painful memories will still be with us, but associated with them forever will be the balm of today's ceremony. We will not think of these abortions and miscarriages the same way again."[1]

Rituals of this type are invaluable for us as we grieve, especially in helping to dispel the guilt we may have carried for years. Rituals allow us to heal the fragmented, or unaccepted, parts of our lives by showing us that we can find the Sacred even in the midst of our failures. This particular ceremony was exceptionally powerful because it involved a group, each woman witnessing to the stories of all the others. Similarly, when we tell our stories to caring friends or in support groups, or when we write the stories out for ourselves, we participate in an elementary healing ritual that can have deep and long-lasting effects.

In Chapter 10 I will speak again about the use of rituals.

ROBIN'S STORY

In his book, *Making Sense of Suffering*, psychologist J. Konrad Stettbacher explains how repressed emotions,

---

[1]Melody Ermachild, "A Ceremony for Lost Children," *Yoga Journal* (November/December, 1991), pp. 106-107.

caused by the lack of genuine comfort we received from parents, can have the effect of driving us, in later life, toward compulsive sexuality, or sex unconscious of the consequences. Not all of us were planned, or wanted, by our parents. Some were just one more unfortunate burden to be dealt with—a required child because the Catholic Church forbade birth control. More and more learn that they were sexually abused by parents or other relatives. Such children receive the clear message that they were bad or guilty for having been such a trial to Mom and Dad, or they internalize a sense of being bad and guilty about the abuse. And they carry that inner ineptness with them into adolescence and adulthood.

Stettbacher quotes a young woman who describes her feelings of being unwanted and the consequences she suffers from that:

> My parents' rejection and disregard for me implanted itself so deeply in me that I no longer understood anything. Every day was a torture of unbearable emotions. I felt I was always in the way—superfluous, useless, inept, and above all, guilty and bad. The effort put into out-maneuvering or evading these feelings left me exhausted. At times I felt like committing suicide, to finally do what my parents had not had the courage to do, although deep inside it was what they all along wanted: to "abort" myself.[2]

The ways in which we attempt to abort ourselves are numerous. For Robin, now age thirty, serious substance abuse was her way of life starting in her late teens. Her story of guilt, fear, and parental rejection at a time when she

[2]J. Konrad Stettbacher, *Making Sense of Suffering* (New York: Dutton, 1991), pp. 83-84.

most needed parental support is a particularly dramatic one. This is the way she explained it:

> When I was about eight years old I started to say to myself, "I never want to have kids." It seemed too painful. One week before my eighteenth birthday I found out that I would always be infertile.
>
> All through high school I felt like a freak because I had no secondary sexual development. No periods. I went through so much pain about it. I was really worried, and fearful, and that came out in shame. I had long hair, and I kept it in front of my chest so that people wouldn't see I had no breasts. Some of the boys in eighth grade used to make comments about my having no shape, and that made things much worse.
>
> My Mom was not supportive. She just said, "Don't worry about it." A few girlfriends knew of my concern, but they couldn't really empathize with the pain of it. I finally took myself to our family doctor to try to find out what was going wrong, and he sent me to several specialists. Then my Mom became angry: she had to drive me around, and to her I was just being a nuisance. I felt guilty, as if it were all my fault. Of course, I'd never speak about it to my Dad. Not even once.
>
> The hospital procedure was called a laparotomy. The physician inserts a device in through the navel, and it allows him to see what's going on. What I learned later was that my ovaries were unformed, and my uterus was only about a centimeter in size. I would never be able to have children.
>
> At the time, however, all I knew was how much pain I was in. I called my Mom from the hospital to tell her that I'd have to stay there an extra day, and

she never even asked me how I was feeling. All she
said was, "Oh, okay, see you tomorrow." My Dad
picked me up without a word. I wanted to cry, but I
didn't. I knew if I did I'd feel like an idiot

When I learned the results of the tests, my Mom
didn't even want to discuss the subject with me. I felt
so much shame. It took me weeks to tell my brother.
He knew I had surgery, but no one ever told him why.

For several days I walked with a cane because I
was in so much pain from the surgical procedure. My
parents never even offered to drive me to school.
There was a complete lack of emotional involvement,
almost total denial, from my family.

I should have expected that response, I suppose.
But I always hoped things would change. When I was
five I broke my arm badly in the supermarket. The
pain was terrible, and I started screaming. My mother told me not to cry, that I was making too much
noise. She was embarrassed. Isn't that incredible?
What self-centeredness. And what a message to give
a kid: "Don't feel. Don't get angry."

Right after my hospital experience I started taking
drugs, drinking alcohol heavily, and eventually abus-
ing myself severely through bulimia. The hormones I
took started changing my body image so radically, so
fast, that I thought I was fat. So I started dieting,
and my mother supported me in that. By the time I
went away to college my eating disorder took off in
full force. I was binging and purging every day—the
perfect way to keep myself in a cycle of guilt, secrecy,
and self-hatred.

Food binges developed ritualistic overtones. I
would plan them and arrange the details of my life
around food. It was common for me to wait until my
roommate was gone and then spend five hours baking

things, eating, and then purging—all extremely secretive. The secrecy increased my feelings of shame and guilt. If my roommate left a pie in the refrigerator that had two pieces out of it, I would eat the whole thing and then rebake an identical pie, eat two pieces out of it, and put it back in the refrigerator. I never knew that other people were doing things like this; I never knew I had a disease; I just knew I hated myself when I did it.

While all this was going on I was extremely active sexually. I felt as if my physical condition gave me a free ticket to sleep around. I just didn't care. It's funny, though, I always felt that I needed to tell my sexual partner about my infertility. I needed to know that he would still accept me because of that.

Shortly after college, I hit bottom. I had no structure. I got a job as a breakfast cook in a college dorm so that I could binge all I wanted. When I couldn't get the jobs I interviewed for, I felt absolutely worthless. I had no self-esteem. To counter this, however, I would exercise compulsively. When I got down to 105 pounds it became a question of life or death. That's when I finally realized I needed help.

It wasn't just the fact of my infertility that precipitated the alcoholism and other abuses. That was only the tip of the iceberg, or the final straw. Now I believe that the whole thing is connected to some early sexual abuse by my grandfather. That pattern is in my family. I'm fairly certain that both my parents were sexually abused, too.

ROBIN'S HEALING

I got help through a variety of twelve-step programs. It has taken years of work to address the issues in my life. My acceptance of my child-free condition is based on the fact that there is nothing I can do about it. Learning to accept the things I cannot change, instead of railing against them, is one of my strongest tools. "This is just the way my body is," I say to myself. No guilt. No blame. I believe there is a reason that I am like this: there is a way I can use this condition to help others, and that it is not a mistake. Now I carry the women's Alcoholics Anonymous message into women's prisons, and I have spoken on television about my recovery from bulimia. These are powerful things for me to do. They make me feel good about myself. I get to see that my suffering was not for nothing. I feel useful, as if I make a difference. I am definitely doing it for me as well as for others.

I don't believe that I need to have children in order to feel whole. But, at times, I do sense the pain of it. I think that I say "I don't want children" because it's still too painful that I can't. I know there is still more grieving for me to do about this, and I'll soon be ready to do this, according to my own timing.

There is a man I care about very much and would like to be closer to. But I know that he wants to have children, and that prevents me from pursuing a relationship with him, and that is a cause of sadness for me. Adoption just isn't in my plan. If I have a child, I want to know that the child came from me. I know how strongly parents influence children, even before birth, and even unconsciously, so I'm not ready to raise somebody else's child.

At work, every other woman on the staff has several children. The topic of conversation is always children: "My child this, my child that." I do feel left out, even though I try to be interested and ask questions, but I recognize it's a subject that I'll never know about.

It's important for me to remember that feelings go up and down and not to get lost when they're on the downward swing. Some days I'm completely accepting, as if my condition were just the right thing for me, and as if I don't need the parenting experience this time around. Then, the next day, if I'm a little low, I use it against myself. "I'm not much of a woman," I might find myself thinking. "If it wasn't for the hormones that I take every day, I wouldn't look like one." Those thoughts trigger that old shame, wanting to hide, judging that my breasts aren't big enough.

But, overall, I feel better about my body. I look around objectively now. There are a lot of small-breasted women around, and they're extremely feminine. I see that.

It has helped tremendously to allow myself to admit to my anger. I was angry at my mother, especially. I was angry at myself. When I stopped the bulimia, the alcoholism, and the drugs, I had rage for almost two years. My support groups allowed me to talk. Outside the group I let myself fume. I wrote all the time, and writing is a constant for me now. My writing lets me identify my feelings—my anger, my underlying sadness and fear. It helps me stay in touch with God, too. Sometimes I write about food. Sometimes I just make gratitude lists to help me to stay out of my negativity. It's really easy for me to slip into that.

Keeping to a disciplined lifestyle has been a crucial factor in my healing. Once I made the decision to stop doing what wasn't healthy for me, my self-esteem increased in all aspects of my life. This type of practice is a lifeline. If I can say "no" to alcohol and dependencies on food, I can say "no" to other things. I

don't have to be swept up in the phony independence
and indulgence of the consumer mentality that says
"I'll do whatever I want." That is a hell-realm. The
cultural message is a lie. It means that I want no limits imposed on me, and that's a fantasy that also oblit-
erates a sense of self-esteem. Spoiled children are
miserable children.

I get down on my knees every day because these
issues are always present to me. My sobriety and
abstinence are a daily, moment-to-moment thing. I
think people are kidding themselves if they think
they're going to do it once and for all.

As for guilt, for the longest time I lived with the
strong feeling of being "defective goods"—a very
common experience for alcoholics. I felt as if I didn't
belong on this planet, as if I was doing something
wrong just by being alive.

Now, when someone approaches me with a guilt
trip or a tone of shaming, I don't buy into it. People
can't shame me unless I let myself be "shameable,"
and that's an important distinction. I don't let the
accusation stick any more. "Hey, you can't treat me
bad without my permission," I say to myself. I'm taking care of me.

Guilt is useless; it does no good. Remorse, on the
other hand, lets me consider what I want to change,
how I want to be different. Part of my sobriety is to
clean up those things that I have made a mess of.

It's interesting that in the last few years I have also
begun to feel more comfortable around children. I'm
no longer afraid that I will scare them away. For a
long time I felt anger toward children, as part of my
anger for not having them. As a result, they stayed
away.

When a child touches me now, or shows that she

accepts me, even likes me, it is like nothing else in the world. A very special gift. I want more of that.

WHERE RESPONSIBILITY BELONGS

When we are able to call things by name we suddenly have some power over them. It's like that with grief in general. Knowing that your emotional and physical responses are normal, you achieve some relief in knowing you aren't completely alone, or crazy.

Naming and making distinctions among guilt, shame, and remorse can be similarly helpful, since change follows awareness. Lots of people walk around suffering and not realizing that there is a way out of the vicious cycle of guilt. After the initial event, guilt becomes not so much a feeling as it is the response to a series of self-defeating inner messages. "I'm bad," the mind repeats. "I could have," it reiterates. "If only," it laments. "I have no one to blame but myself," it affirms. It's as if the mind gets stuck in a tape-loop, replaying the situations that created the bad feelings and repeating these messages of condemnation over and over again. Once you begin to identify your tendency to feed guilt or shame (which will almost always take you down a useless path), you can begin to work with it.

While we tend to use the words interchangeably, guilt and shame can be distinguished. Guilt follows a belief or fear that we have done something "bad" or "wrong," either deliberately or accidentally. The guilt may be for some action, or nonaction, either real or imagined—the actual circumstances are often not the issue. Some people will feel tremendous guilt about something that others feel is a small matter. It all depends upon one's relationship to the situation and one's tendency to use anything available to reinforce unworthiness.

With shame there is a sense of embarrassment at having been discovered in some "immoral" or socially unaccept-
able behavior. So shame arises from the reactions or presence of others. Shame, like guilt, is learned and built.
Children don't have these responses until they are taught.
And for that same reason, they can be unlearned, or at least
relegated to a less dominant place in the psyche.

For Robin, part of healing from the guilt of her life
amounted to realizing that her guilt and shame were instilled
initially by the culture, by her parents, and by insensitive
companions. It is central to the issue of guilt and shame to
be able to admit that we didn't ask for such guilt-ridden messages and to be able to place the responsibility for those
early lessons where they belong. That doesn't mean we need
to blame our parents or anyone else. It means that we give
them back the responsibility for what we have been carrying
around and blaming ourselves with for so long. Telling our
stories helps us do that.

Story-telling and journal writing can also help us to
put our guilt into the perspective of the here-and-now. "If I
knew then that I would never have children, I would never
have chosen to give up my child for adoption," said one
woman. But, the point is, she couldn't know that at the
time. No one could. Not even God.

In cases where our actions have hurt others, objectively, I think it's wiser to choose a word other than "guilt"—
even if you call it "healthy guilt" as some writers about
grief tend to do. I would rather assert that guilt is not
helpful, ever. Instead, I suggest using the word "remorse."

Sol, a well-respected businessman, shared the remorse
he felt about the way he parented his stepdaughters. Years
later, his ruthless self-honesty and remorse helped him to
radically change his approach to his own children.

My stepdaughters were six and four when I first got

involved in their lives. When they were that age
things were relatively good with us, but the older they
got the more repressive I got as a parent. I wanted
them to do things my way. "You'll thank me later,"
was my attitude.

Our relationship deteriorated gradually. I was definitely not available to who they were. According to
me, I was right and they were wrong. It is painful to
look back and realize that.

I estranged myself from my stepdaughters by
being critical of their heroes, their lifestyles, their
music. And I was constantly moralizing. It was a
petty way to be, and certainly not supportive of their
personhood. My unconsciousness was extremely hyp-
ocritical because at the same time I was teaching a
self-improvement course about consciousness.

Sure, I was frustrated by the lack of communication.
I wasn't stupid. I knew it wasn't all their fault. I was
frustrated with myself as well as with the situation.

My relationship with the girls is still painful and
sore. The remorse I felt about them really helped me
to relate differently to my own son years later—adult-
to-adult, rather than authority-to-ward. That
remorse transformed me. I really didn't have to be
careful not to repeat those rigid patterns with my son.
I was just different. When I was with him, I reinforced all his positive qualities as much as I could.

One of the best things I ever did was to give him an
electric guitar and an amplifier. I knew he loved his
music. He would play for five or six hours a day, and
honestly it disturbed everybody in the house. But I
asked them to be patient. I figure that, if someone
finds something he or she loves, let the noise go on.
So I put up with it. It gave him something he couldn't
have gotten any other way.

Remorse can be a helpful feeling, one that inspires us to "clean up our act," as Robin said—one that drives us to the edge of what it means to be a human being. How else will we know the uncountable mercies of God unless we are willing to admit the places in which we have fallen short of our ideal? Letting ourselves feel the pain of such unactualized potential—that is, unactualized love—without turning that pain in upon ourselves, but just because that is the human condition, can open us to the wise innocence that is our underlying reality.

FOR JOURNALLING

At the end of each of our interviews, Susan and I would ask the grieving person to tell us what she or he would say to another man or woman in the same situation. Always, the advice was full of compassion. Often, it contained a specific message about the uselessness of guilt.

The following writing exercise is structured to help you gain a little distance from your own guilt feelings, your own harsh self-judgements. It will encourage you to look with compassion on another person who is going through the same grief you are experiencing. Here's what to do:

1. Reflect upon any aspects of your loss that you still feel guilty or bad about.

2. Imagine that your best friend had gone through your exact situation and was feeling guilty and bad about it in the same way you are. Ask yourself how you would reach out to her or him. What would you say that would make a difference?

3. Now write that "guilty friend" a letter in which you express your support and consolation. Tell her or him what you know to be true about the guilt, even if you can't quite put it into practice for yourself yet.

4. At the conclusion of your writing, read back over what you have written. Then summarize what you are feeling or thinking by completing the following phrase: As a result of doing this writing I. . . .

If you are inspired to continue writing about any aspects of your loss, even if not related specifically to guilt, you can trust that inspiration. Keep writing.

6

It's Out of My Hands

We are always losing something—we have to. It's necessary to leave behind what *was* in order to experience what *is* or what *could be*. But most of the time our losses are so natural, so much connected to the developmental cycle, that we barely give attention to them. Only when the evidence has accumulated beyond our power to dismiss, as it does on the fateful day when those few faint lines around our eyes turn into full-fledged wrinkles, does the reality come home to roost. Only when faced with something that is beyond our control do we feel the frustration, the sadness, the pain of this life of loss.

Deborah and her husband felt this powerlessness when faced with the challenge of dealing with infertility.

She told us:

> We have always been completely achievement-oriented
> people, but with this we ran up against a brick wall.
> People in our situation commonly feel as if they've lost
> control of their own bodies, and that's very frustrating.
> We don't like it. We don't want it. We don't want our
> sex life to be determined by the calendar. We don't
> want to have to make one more hard decision. And we
> especially don't want to think that something so closely
> connected to our sense of being a competent, self-deter-
> mining adult is really out of our hands.

Intellectualization is one of the primary ways that people try to cope with a situation that feels out of control. They
educate themselves about it—to the point where they are
conversant with it at a level of sophistication that even their
medical specialists sometimes fear. This strategy is helpful,
in the short run, but sooner or later it also keeps them from
facing feelings that will need to be dealt with. It can easily
become another subtle form of denial.

The grief associated with loss of our children through
custody settlements is another case in which powerlessness
shows up. We may think that we tried our very best, that we
gave at least fifty percent, but when the judgement that is
rendered is not in our favor, we know the pain of powerlessness. When we see our children being raised in ways that we
do not approve, we feel helpless to make a change.

Feeling somewhat powerless in relationship to children
is a common experience for parents. For some, however, circumstances arise in which they feel overwhelmed by helplessness, as if they have lost their children completely.
Witness the pain of those parents whose children are no
longer spiritually or emotionally available to them because of
drug or alcohol abuse, involvement in a cult, a pattern of running away, constant tension with the law, or confinement to

prison or reform school. How does one resolve the guilt and sense of helplessness that accompanies the knowledge that one's child was raped or molested by another family member or a stranger? What of the powerlessness we face with our adopted children who have never bonded to us, our own children who are resentful of not living with their other parent, or our stepchildren who tyrannize us with the assurance that we will never live up to the ideal of their "real Dad" or "real Mom"? What of the powerlessness beyond powerlessness that occurs when a child dies?

These are the issues that cloud the lives of millions of us, smashing our false expectations of the idyllic nature of parenthood and forcing us to confront our helplessness, our lack of control, our brokenness, compounded by the vast brokenness of the society in which we live and out of which many of our problems emerge.

Grief destroys illusions: the illusion that we can fix everything, the illusion that we are ultimately in charge, the illusion that we can have it all. That's hard to take. All of a sudden our previous strategies for keeping these illusions in place are swept out from under us and leave us feeling rootless.

Grief like this can be especially difficult for men. Their world is constructed around work and power—around achieving, providing, fixing. Men, in this culture, have less permission for the expression of vulnerability and emotionality—a great handicap in the process of adequate mourning. While there may be a sliver of openness in the culture for acknowledging the plight of the grieving woman, particularly a mother, few if any compassionate myths relate to the losses suffered by men or fathers.

I discovered that there are differences in the ways in which many men (in contrast to women) process and integrate the pain of their lives during these critical transitions. It seems that some of their issues *are* unique to their sex, and that these issues are uncovered only as men begin to speak the story of their grief—their feelings of insanity, powerlessness, and helplessness—as they wrestle, some for the very first time, with this ruthlessly demanding demon called "loss."

THE MIDWIFE'S STORY

Johanna, the midwife who has assisted many of my friends in birthing their children, shared a lot about the powerlessness that men suffer when a pregnancy terminates or a child dies.

> Any loss of a child is, I think, more confusing for a man than it is for a woman because of the pervasive attitudes toward the male's role in childraising. Pregnancy and infancy care are thought of as female jobs. It can be terribly hard, then, for a man to figure out where he is in all of this.
>
> Women have hormones that help bring out the maternal instinct, whether the pregnancy turns out to be viable or not. For a woman there is bodily proof that something is happening—that is, she feels the baby growing in her. But not so for the man, which is why I witness so many "gender-gap" conflicts during pregnancy, and especially when the pregnancy is lost. A woman wants her man to feel the excitement, or the fear, or the devastating loss in the same ways that she feels it. She wants it to be as important to him as it is to her.
>
> What she really desires, overall, is his involvement. But the poor guy is at a distinct disadvantage. It's not that real to him. He knows that she's throwing up in the morning, that she's peeing a lot more, and there's all this talk about a baby. And he knows on the level of logic that, yes, he's going be a father in the near future. But he doesn't have the advantage of these

hormones to make him think in a certain way and feel in a certain way. So he tends to miss out.

When there is a miscarriage early in the pregnancy, and a lot of times even later in the pregnancy, the man's concern is generally more for his wife than it is for the baby. He may have no true feelings of loss yet. Most men, I think, believe that the baby is real only when they can hold it, and generally not before.

Miscarriage presents a real conflict for a man because he wants to feel what his wife or partner feels. Especially when there is a loss, he wants to feel it so that he can share it fully with her and support her in the way she needs to be supported. But it's just too different an experience for each of them.

When his friend Tom's baby died, Redhawk, a poet friend of mine, composed this piece as a gift. It touches upon some of the pain and challenge a man faces with such a loss.

FOR TOM, WHOSE BABY DIED

It is hard for a man
because he does not have the comfort
of hard labor and bodily pain,
of something to be done.

His only solace
is the quiet touch
of his hand on her cheek,
of his eyes humbly sharing with her

an unbearable Love.
He does not give her too much;
his strength comes from the art
of when to look away,

when to remain silent,
when to leave her alone.
He grows by diminishing self.
He serves her in a way

that does not show, that supports
with hidden hand;
and in so doing, he also serves Another
whose heartbeat is a trace

between them, whose breath
he feels on his face
at night
as she turns to softly hold him.

It is a kind of grace
given to a man whose child dies:
that he can humbly labor then,
that he can suffer himself

to bear the heartbeat of his child
and deliver it into the world
as kindness, as service to others,
as humble work done without reward.

PETER'S STORY

An example of a man's grief is portrayed dramatically in
Peter's story. Although he never had any children of his own,
losing his partner's children through divorce and separation
pushed him up against the pain of being helpless and out of
control.

I have been in two long-term relationships. One
ended in divorce, the next in separation. In both cases
children were involved. The separation from my
female partner was terrible. The separation from the
kids was, in each case, devastating.
I have such a protective feeling about family and

what it means to really take care of a spouse and children. That feeling came up in both separations. It is a very specific pain, of knowing that a woman and children that you love are out there in the world but you can no longer look after them. All the self-judgements about failure that are connected with a separation are essentially psychological: what I'm talking about is something instinctive—it's very different. When I was with my partner and children, I was there in the role of a man attempting to create a safe place for his family. Yes, safety. That's exactly the word. When that role is lost, it can drive a man crazy.

The breaking of this bond between men and children, between man and woman, is very painful, and it really doesn't end. I remember that a year after our breakup, my ex-wife and step-daughter were living in Santa Cruz, and I was in Los Angeles. When the earthquake hit Santa Cruz and I found out about it, I panicked. "Jeannie, Sara, they're not safe." It was as if they had never left me.

I am ashamed to say that I never really understood what children meant, beyond the personal attachment, until my separation. Children haven't lost their innocence, and this innocence is precious and important to be close to. I miss that so much. Children bring life into life.

Life is for kids. Being able to contribute to them makes going out making a living worthwhile. I am still building my business in the hope that I can get back to them. A man without his family is just a vagabond. He has no power. I felt as if I got kicked out of the universe. When a woman kicks you out of her world, you are kicked out of the universe.

These separations have been the most painful events of my life. I built a wall against the pain by asserting intellectually that most things were okay.

But one feeling I did let in: I did allow myself to feel
hatred for my partner. Maybe people will be shocked
to read that, but it's true. I wish it hadn't happened,
but I did hate her for a long time. I hated her for
using the children as a way to get back at me. I hated
her for taking them away from me. They wanted to
be with me, and I'm sure she had convinced them that
they didn't. I was good to them, and I am very angry
that she refuses to see that I am committed to them.

When you bond with children, having them
wrenched away is just unfair. When women do this to
men I think they don't realize how devastating it is.
My partner hasn't lost the whole family, but I have.
She still has the intimacy of family; I have nothing. I
don't think that women understand what it means to
the man. It is so hard. These kids were my family,
even though I wasn't their biological father.

I've talked to many other fathers who are going
through divorce, or who live apart from their kids for
years. Especially when the kids are young, it never
gets easy to take them back to Mom on Sunday afternoon. Dropping them off always leaves a big hole.

It must be especially hard if men don't have male
friends, the way I do. Without a support system, it
must be intolerable. This loss of children and father-
hood has got to be one of the deepest pains that a man
could feel. I can see why we have a society of men
who abuse women and children. Men often don't know
how to deal with their powerlessness except through
alcoholism or violence. A lot of men's frustration is
about not having a choice. The male ideal is to run the
world and have choice. Custody rights is one of the
few areas of life in which women consistently win
against men. At last the woman gets to say, "This time
I'm in control!" It's one of the few ways that she has

of getting back at the man. That is really significant.

My two ex-mates still have an ironclad list of grievances against me—about what I did and what I didn't do. I just can't win. Even if I try to change, they are in so much pain that they will interpret what I do in some other way. The woman therefore puts a wall up against the man. I'm not saying that men don't have a lot of work to do to really be present in a relationship. They do. But at some point a woman's got to forgive.

WOMEN'S GRIEF, AND POWER

The crisis of meaning that men experience in losing something important shows itself in many different ways, the most irrefutable being the high suicide rate among our young male population. And while young women generally don't kill themselves at the alarming rate that young men do, the correspondingly high number of unwanted pregnancies and abortions may well be connected to a similar sense of powerlessness and angst.

Teenage pregnancy and unconscious pregnancy is, I believe, often a cry for help—a way to restablish meaning in a life that feels out of control. For a woman, knowing that she has the power to conceive a child may bring another fleeting moment of self-affirmation to an otherwise disempowered life. Shelley, a young divorced woman and mother of two, spoke about the way her fantasy of marriage crumbled when she found no relief from her personal pain and low self-esteem. "I had a thing about cranking out babies," she confessed shyly. "I thought: If only I create more things to nurture, I will be better. I just needed to know that I had this ability to have babies and to be pregnant. Pregnancy awakened my own sense of innocence, and it gave me confir-

mation that I was still alive when, for so much of the rest of
the time, I was in denial about so many things."

Having spoken with many women who had children or
abortions during their teenage years, I am convinced that
young, pregnant daughters are trying to tell their mothers
something, trying to reclaim something, trying to get out of
their mothers' houses and into their own. Yet, more often
than not, the cry for help is not heard. Instead, the circumstances of the pregnancy are only cause for more pain, and
soon a complex situation becomes convoluted. The woman's
unconscious plan has in fact backfired. Now she doesn't
know what she is grieving. Is it the pregnancy, the abortion,
the loss of mother, the loss of self? Or is it all of the above?

For many women, powerlessness was (or still is) inherent in their lifestyle. A woman is, therefore, much less a
stranger to loss than her mate or partner is. Especially in
issues of birth or death, a woman comes face to face continu-
ously with patriarchal establishments—churches, hospitals,
educational systems—that claim to have her "best interests
at heart" while they functioning unconsciously to disempow-
er her relationship to her own body and her intuitive wisdom. In much the same way that our natural innocence has
been sapped from our childhood, our relationship to our bodies as a source of knowledge and healing has been eroded
through a glorification of, and reliance on, order, cost-effec-
tiveness, and technology. For many, it has meant the relega-
tion of birth and death to a sterile, prison-like environment.
Even in the best of times, it is difficult to stand up against
powerful cultural norms. When women are faced with
deeply personal decisions or shocked by unforeseen realities,
they are even less likely to have the strength to say "No," or
at least, "Wait a minute, please."

Yet shocking circumstances are frequently the call to
our awakenings. The trauma of losing a child or a relationship with a child becomes, for many women, a rite of pas-

sage—an initiation into profound grief and therefore into a deeper level of self-understanding. Marion Woodman has written that for most women, initiation into their own individuality comes through their bodies.

> Through sexuality, through love or loss of love, through having a child or not having a child, through illness, they are suddenly invaded by the mystery of power over which they have no control. They are forced to surrender to their individual destiny.[1]

CONNIE'S STORY

Connie, a friend of Susan's and mine, spent years living behind a veil of powerlessness before being able to face her true feelings. An abortion early in her marriage rent the relationship with her husband in ways that were never fully repaired. Yet, as Marion Woodman implies is the situation for many, the abortion was also a rite of passage for Connie—an entry into a deeper level of suffering than she had known before. In her interview, Connie was able to speak about her initiation through her pain, to weep for the time she had lost, and to express her relief in sharing her story in a way that helped her to accept and integrate it.

> A few months after I was married I started feeling sick every day, and didn't understand why. It honestly never dawned on me that I might be pregnant.
>
> Everything about my body was changing; even my contact lenses wouldn't fit. But I still never put two and two together. After I finally got an exam, the doctor called me into his office, leaned back in his big leather chair and smiled. "Well," he said, placing his

---

[1]Marion Woodman, *Leaving My Father's House* (Boston: Shambhala, 1992), p. 210.

fingertips together the way people do when they are
discussing a big decision, "it's very simple. You're
pregnant." I remember reaching out and touching the
edge of that smooth wooden desk, and then holding
onto it. I was completely shocked. Speechless.
Really, I almost fell down out of my chair. It was all
so sudden, and I wasn't planning it.

Somehow, I got home that day and when I saw my
husband, Scott, I just blurted it out. His response
shocked me. "I thought you might have been. I had a
hunch," he said coolly, and with such a superior attitude. I was infuriated. "Why didn't you tell me?" I
screamed at him. I just couldn't believe his attitude.
I had been pregnant for quite a while. In fact, it was
right at the border of the time when a woman can get
an abortion.

Instantly, my husband's reaction was to take control. (What a man!) "This is the situation," he began
in his "I've got it all together" tone. "And this is how
we are going to handle it," he went on. Well, I was a
newly-married woman at the time, and I was scared,
confused, all of it. So I never thought to question his
judgement. Before we were married we had "worked
out" that we weren't going to have children. Actually,
he was adamant about that because he already had
two children by a previous marriage. But I had never
explored the option emotionally. It's one thing to
make a decision about this before it happens, but it's
another once the child is actually there.

What does a woman do? I was in my early twenties, feeling that this "problem" was somehow my
fault, not wishing to cause conflict by suggesting that
we keep the pregnancy. All my neurotic, pressured
excuses finally led only to an appointment for an abortion.

That was the decision, and I went through with it.
The hospital people were very kind, thank God. But
it was terrible nonetheless. I can still feel the machine
of the "D and C." I can hear it. It sucks everything
out of your body. Even then, I was so aware that
something was living inside of me. Sure, it wasn't
very well-formed, but it had its own life. It wasn't
just a wart on my skin, or like losing my hair. The
matrix for "somebody else" was being formed. I'm
still incredulous that it happened and that I agreed to
it, insisting that I didn't want children.

As I realize it now, I think it was my mother, not I,
who didn't want a child.

Emotionally, I was for a long time in a state of
shock. Things seemed very flat, and I thought to
myself, "Well, I guess I don't have strong feelings." It
didn't seem permissible at the time to feel these feelings. A long time later, months or years, I remembered it all again. Then I spent a whole night crying
for the loss of that child.

Scott made it very clear that he didn't want to
know about what I was going through. It wasn't as if
he was nasty about it; no, not at all. It was all very
cut-and-dried. "Clearly," he was saying, "you are
there and I am here, and we'll do all these things
together, but when you want to be a woman and have
all these plans, do not step over these lines and be
emotional."

This situation marked the beginning of the end for
us, even though our marriage endured for almost
twenty years. But after his responses to my pain I
didn't know how to pursue tenderness with him.
Instead, I frequently exploded at him with anger and
frustration. These were the only ways we had to
relate. My pain had to come out in some form.

Nor did I share anything at all with my mother. With her, too, I could never be intimate. She, too, had made clear for years that she couldn't handle hearing these kinds of things.

So it was a very lonely time for me. I had no real woman friends at the time, since we had just moved. Later, we developed a social circle, and then I was able to spend time talking about what had happened to me. But mostly, I did my grieving alone.

Late at night it would happen. The pain would wash over me, touching me deeply. And I would allow myself to feel it, and I never felt wrong about that. In fact, I actually felt closer to God in those moments. That kind of pain connected me to some broader perspective. I think it tapped me into knowing that nothing I could possess would every really satisfy me. I knew that having a child would not do it, either, especially if I would make a child into a possession.

Shortly after that, Scott had a vasectomy. He never asked me about it; it was completely his decision. That was another shock. I would like to have considered it with him. His decision meant that I would never have children, since at that point I couldn't see beyond my relationship to him. Earlier, I had thought to myself, "Maybe I will some day change my mind, and perhaps have the emotional stability to bear a child." But his vasectomy changed all that. It slammed the door in my face.

I suppose I should have seen it then—that we would never really be happy together. But instead I just took it all and often felt guilty, as if I had done something bad. The first eight years of our marriage I held on for dear life. The last eight years I was plotting my way out of there. Certainly, I had spurts of enthusiasm and even love, but the seeds of "this is not working" were growing. I would occasionally become panicked, thinking that I would never have a child or never have another relationship with a man.

That abortion happened almost twenty years ago, and yet every once in a while it still hits me. I see another woman with a child, and I feel it. I look at the body clock and realize that it's ticking away and that it won't be long before I will pass childbearing age. But I also see that childbearing is not something that I want to force to happen.

This is a very sad and significant part of my life, and it cannot be undone. I would honor new life if I were fortunate enough to conceive again, and it is a consideration for me. Still.

ADVICE TO OTHERS?

Near the end of her time with us, I asked Connie to consider what she would tell another woman in a situation similar to hers. Here is what she told us:

If I knew another woman was really going to consider abortion, I couldn't support the decision, but I couldn't turn away from *her*. I would simply try hard to communicate what I had learned—how it all seemed, at the time, like a very rational decision, because my mind was like that, too. "Who needs to bring another child into the world, if it is only going to be treated as my mother treated me?" That's the way the mind works.

I wouldn't try to change her mind, but I would want to offer the other side of the coin: the benefit of my twenty years of working with it. I think that something else needs to be considered here, beyond the notions of "I want the baby" or "I don't want the baby." Abortion is more than simply a personal issue.

I would encourage any woman to speak about her pain or tell her story. To write about it, too, is very helpful. Doing these things have brought me closer to the pain of others, feeling their losses and knowing that we must all reconcile ourselves with the decisions we have made in our lives.

We are not supposed to forget, just acknowledge and feel. Suffering brings one to earth, to the dust and ashes of feeling into a sorrow that everyone carries—the suffering of thinking that we are separate from God. But that is too much to think about, especially at first. These everyday pains are enough. The sorrow of our lives—the pain of losing something, the pain of missing something—that we can feel. That's where we have to start.

SUPPORT: THE REMEDY FOR POWERLESSNESS

Powerlessness is a heavy weight to carry alone, even though we try. In time of need, our strategies for proving that we can take care of ourselves usually only add to our loneliness and sense of frustration. In the long-term, there is no substitute for relationships with other people. The embracing arms, or soothing words, or simply the silent presence of another human being is a lifeline that connects us with reality and affirms that we are not without resources, especially at a time when we have forgotten this for ourselves.

Friends of the same sex can be a particularly valuable resource as we are grieving. Men need to know from other men that their emotions are acceptable. A man's pain runs deep. As Susan and I interviewed men for this book, we consistently heard from them, sometimes between the lines, sometimes directly, their aching need to share their pain with the members of their own sex. Some, like Mitch, an older father, had additional insight into the value of men using other men for support.

> When I was going through divorce and the custody proceedings for my first two sons, I was more drawn toward women for help and consolation. Despite my anger and aggressiveness towards women, I still used them for support. I believed that I could relate better to women than to men. A lot of men say this, and I hear women saying that they relate better to men. But the truth is that we're scared of how much we see and know about our own kind, so we avoid them.
>
> It was easy for me to manipulate a woman with my suffering and to pull the wool over her eyes. But I couldn't do that with men. They knew exactly what I was up to immediately, and even though it's hard to hear the truth, still, it's a relief. I never really got how messed up I was until my male friends helped me admit this.
>
> It's very hard for men to open up. We all have a lot of resistance and fear in being together. But when we do, it's great.

As men need men, women need other women during times of loss. Women need to hear that they can trust themselves. They need to be able to speak about the intimacies of their own bodies, their birthing processes, their difficult decisions, to those who know what it means to have a female body.

We all need to be reminded that we will survive and find the light, as dark as the current tunnel seems to be. Those who have walked this path before us are the ideal ones to guide our faltering steps. (See the section on emotional help and support groups in Chapter 10.)

PETER'S HEALING PROCESS

Peter's story, which you read earlier, continues here. In discussing the ways in which he healed and grew from his loss of children through separation and divorce, Peter's words echo those of Mitch, testifying to the invaluable support he received, particularly from his male friends.

For me it is essential to do anything I can in order not to lose touch with my feelings. Men, in my experience, either fixate on anger or on feeling nothing at all. They don't let themselves feel scared, sad, or joyful, and these feelings are necessary for their healing.

The way I keep from going numb is to spend time alone, undistracted. No television, no videos, no beer. Then the feelings will naturally come up. I also spend time with men friends who are willing to talk about our feelings. Even though I have good women friends, I recognize that it is really hard not to be "gamey" with them. They will play mother to me, or I will be asking them subtly to be mother for me.

I had to admit that I'd lost. That was a big one for me. But I needed to face the pain of that. When things got intolerable, it was helpful to remember that I was not in control of life and that rewards and punishments are left to the powers that be. They will handle it, although maybe not in the way I would like.

Using other men is important. Often, when I am feeling overwhelmed about some aspect of my grief, or when I come up with some ultimatum that I am going to level at my ex-wife or partner, I will call a male friend. He helps me to keep some sense of objectivity when I lose it, and you can bet that I still lose it a lot. But that problem is lessening over time.

It is surprising to learn that men often spend more time, and better quality time, with their kids after their divorce or separation than before. It was for me. That realization can provoke a lot of remorse, and there is no way around that pain except just to face it. The society we live in is a big part of the problem. Men are not supported in being available to their kids. So I try not to blame myself for all of that.

I work hard now not to use the children to fill the emptiness in myself or to cover up my pain. Instead, I try to be there to serve them as completely as I can.

I've been able to use the opportunity as an initiation into manhood. The author Robert Bly says that initiation involves some sort of betrayal and then forgiveness. Men and women have betrayed each other, I think. If a woman could forgive a man, she would become a Woman. If a man could forgive a woman, he would become a Man.

BOB'S HEALING

In Chapter Four I recorded the story of Bob, who felt out of control and wondered if he were going crazy. Here I include the completion of his narrative, which tells of his healing resources and reinforces the theme of this chapter: powerlessness.

I really like being with the children now, even though I am only a weekend father. At first, of course, I wanted them all the time. Now I'm grateful for whatever I have. This "father thing" is not something you can define in words or quantify in time. It's way beyond that. So now I simply recognize and live with my wound. And, yes, it makes you more mature, but you don't necessarily have to wear that on your sleeve.

This whole painful process has connected me in a more ordinary way to my spiritual life. It realigned all my priorities. I was making a lot of money, but it was clear to me that money wasn't the point.

Men friends are so valuable at these junctures! A man I had known only casually, a guy named Rick, all of a sudden was there as a part of my support system, and we became really close friends. He had gone through a divorce and was willing to be completely open to me about it. He spoke straight, in a way that I could hear. "Take care of your needs," he said in his matter-of-fact style, "because no one else will, and you need to attend to your needs most of all right now." A lot of men, I think, don't relate to the concept of having needs, except maybe for sex. But that is only a very limited part of the picture. We have more important needs for friendship and a sense of self-worth. Having someone who has been through it say these things to me was extremely nurturing.

I started to genuinely miss my other men friends a lot and soon got into the habit of calling my brother almost every day. That was a saving grace. Even if I didn't have anything to talk about, I just needed to hear a voice, a caring voice. These daily talks with my brother saved my life. I would just soak up every word.

And now that I've started on my path of healing, I'm noticing that other men are coming to me in the same ways. When I see that someone is getting something from me, I want to give more. Of course, a lot of men are so out of touch that they can't even realize that they could use me.

I pray that I am finished with my patterns of trying to blame other people for the things that haven't worked out for me. I hope I am no longer going to make others wrong.

My advice to other men in my situation is: Don't try to get even, for whatever reason. Minimize the backlash. Do not make a big deal, even though your situation feels like the end of the world. Dramatizing things just makes it harder on the children. Go through this process as elegantly as you can, for the children. They need you at times like this. Draw your strength from wherever you can get it. If you need to have an affair, then do it if that will keep you sane for your children. Be the best father you can be. Don't argue with your former wife or partner if you can possibly avoid it.

If it *is* the end of the world, the suffering you go through will broaden your horizons. The waves of grief that follow are just what come with the territory. Go to a safe space and cry. Find someone who you can be vulnerable with, and be with that person. You won't be able to figure out exactly went wrong, or why these things are happening to you, even though you will try like hell to do so. The pain is like love. It is not figure-out-able. And that's hard for men to accept because many of us learned that the intellect was the important thing. Well, the intellect isn't running the show when you lose a child. You *never* make sense of it.

All things are transitory. You won't believe it at the time, because when you have a bad toothache, that's all you can think about. But your pain can also be a tremendous reminding factor—a time when you remember God, or remember where you came from or what you're on earth to do. When you're in pain you remember to listen to the raindrops. When you're not in pain you are afraid of getting wet.

We are always trying to dodge our suffering. But when you lose your children, lose your wife, lose your role as father and husband, your identity, you are faced with a situation in which you can't totally block out the pain. That's when you have your heart bro-

ken. I really believe that you are never given more
suffering than you can take. The body and mind are
really merciful; they close down when they can't handle something.

The world is full of pain. We need to face that. And
if you can grab a little happiness along the way, do it.
If you can give love, give it. That is the only weapon
you have. Suffering is a teacher, and life is good even
though some days are just plain shitty.

Human beings are also incredibly resilient. Don't
forget that. You will survive.

I saw Bob about a year after this interview and felt how
strongly he was living his own advice. His sensitivity,
warmth, and caring were clearly evident to me. Bob is a man
who is constantly being transformed by suffering. He's
worked hard for that privilege.

FOR JOURNALLING

I opened this chapter by pointing out that loss is inherent in every aspect of life. When people reflect on the many
losses they have experienced throughout their lives, they not
only mourn but also come to appreciate loss as a necessary
dynamic in evolution, both personal and planetary.

1. One way to see the place of loss in the bigger picture of your life is to chart your life on a "time line"
   and mark the significant events or times of loss
   that you have gone through.

   Another way to do that is to designate specific
   time periods, such as childhood, grade school years,
   high school and adolescent years, and to list under
   each time period the things or people you can
   remember losing or grieving at that time.

   For example: In my childhood I lost: (fill in your
   losses).

2. With regard to your child-related loss and the sense of powerlessness that is common with that, use the following incomplete sentences to expand your personal awareness, to specify some of your generalized feelings of anxiety, and to remind yourself once again of your resources. Try to complete these sentences in as many ways as you can, with five or more responses for each one.

I feel helpless or out of control about. . . .

- When I feel helpless or out of control, I. . . .
- Real help is. . . .
- I can get real help. . . .

Go on to write about anything that occurs to you now, for as long as you wish.

3. Conclude your journalling experience by responding to the following:
As a result of doing this writing, I. . . .

7

It's Not Fair

*Down, down, down into the darkness
of the grave
Gently they go, the beautiful, the tender, the kind;
Quietly they go, the intelligent, the
witty, the brave.
I know. But I do not approve. And I
am not resigned.*

FROM "DIRGE WITHOUT MUSIC"
BY EDNA ST. VINCENT MILLAY

IT'S UNFAIR that children should die, that they should be separated from their parents, that they should be made a part of a divorce settlement. Any loss of a child upsets the balance and rightness of things. The young and the innocent should not have to suffer, and loving parents should not have to lose their children! Anger and resentment are the natural outcomes of facing such injustice or helplessness. "I am not resigned," says the poet, hitting the nail on the head.

Anger and resentment are not pretty emotions. They

sometimes cause people to act out, with loud voices in quiet places. When was the last time you heard someone wail or scream in a hospital? Usually, that kind of behavior is quickly sedated or the offending party quickly removed.

Elisabeth Kubler-Ross, who pioneered the contemporary approaches to grief work, suggested that every hospital should ideally be equipped with a "scream-room"—a safe place where patients and their families could go to release, vocally, their pent-up emotional energy, particularly anger and sadness. That idea always intrigued me. Many of my students have reported on the therapeutic value of screaming or wailing. Some have done their screaming in their parked cars; others have used an isolated place in nature; many simply scream into their pillows.

Unfortunately, it is still necessary to search out an isolated or safe place to express anger or sometimes even sadness. While there is more tolerance and understanding for men to show their anger, there is almost none for women. "Nice little girls" are not supposed to get angry. We've been trained for generations to put up with pain and injustice with a smile. We can cry, but if we ever rage we run the risk of being assigned the consummate insult of being labeled "a bitch." So, when our world has been shattered and we look for some way to revenge it, we face a difficult quandary.

THE OBJECTS OF OUR ANGER

Angry people tend to lash out against perceived injustice. We look for a scapegoat—someone to blame for the unfair situation. At such times it is common for anger to be directed at anyone and everyone who crosses our path but especially at those whom we judge responsible for the tragedy we are experiencing. That can easily include our physicians, our caregivers, our friends and spouses who attempt to offer help, our ministers, priests, and rabbis who attempt to supply us with meaning. Anger can focus on the insurance company that doesn't cover our expenses or the newspaper that doesn't cover our story. Anger and resentment can flare up unexpectedly at other people who are enjoying their children or at our children themselves for the grief they have caused us.

When that anger is directed at God, as it frequently is, it can be particularly disturbing to the person who feels it and to friends and family members who are shocked by it. But as Kubler-Ross, in her ageless wisdom, again reminds us, who can take it better than God?

The insensitivities of others, whether they are deliberately cruel, unconscious, or merely curious, can evoke tremendous rage, sometimes enough to frighten us.

Shortly after learning that her five-month-old fetus was no longer viable, but before she miscarried, Jean felt the sting of invasive curiosity. In a letter to me she wrote:

> As I grabbed the handle of the sliding-glass patio door, a visitor stood expectantly in my path. A neighbor. An acquaintance of my husband's, actually. "Oh, hi, Bill," I said, somewhat startled. "Gary just left for class, and I'm late for an appointment." I talked about nothing in particular as we walked to the parking lot.
>
> Leaning on our mile-long station wagon Bill abruptly pierced the welcome silence with, "Jean, when did *you*, not the doctor, first recognize that something was wrong?" Bill's assertive tone hung in the air like that of a roving television reporter on assignment.
>
> I was shocked and outraged by his intrusive, insensitive interview. Here they come (I thought), those

invisible bands pressing relentlessly around my head
and gouging into my temple. Adrenalin pumped
through me in burning streams of chaotic energy. I
felt dizzy and nauseous—and trapped. In the question I heard only callous curiosity, no heart, no safe
place to connect with a fellow human.

As I finally dropped woodenly into the driver's seat
and noticed absently that Bill was still standing there
waiting for a response, I dismissed him with an arm
motion to move out of the way as I swung out of the
parking place.

Jean had a target for her rage and a way to act on it. If
she hadn't, she might have directed the anger internally,
blaming herself for being so reactive or for putting herself in
such a vulnerable situation. She may have attempted to
swallow it completely. The numbness that many people
report during times of grief is often the result of repressed
anger. Depression, in my experience, is a consequence of
unexpressed emotion, including anger.

In general, it is healthier to acknowledge anger or
resentment, even if you don't express it actively, than to sti-
fle it. When anger is not dealt with it is particularly insidious
in the way it affects the health of the body. My partner John
Travis, M.D., writes about "a woman who had chronic ure-
thral strictures and had to be dilated mechanically every
month or so because she couldn't urinate. In the (therapeutic) group she realized that she wanted to 'piss on' her husband, but never expressed her anger. When she started
communicating her feelings, the problem cleared up." John
goes to on to say: "I know of problems of impotence, menstrual cramps, infertility and VD which have all been related
to deep-seated, unexpressed feelings," particularly around a
person's sexuality. While John is not denying the necessity
for medical attention, he is strongly advocating that "in con-

junction with treatment we look at the unexpressed feelings that may have brought on the condition."[1]

Many people deny or repress anger because they have catastrophic expectations that expressing it will mean the onset of some type of violent behavior. That is not the case. Anger can be expressed in safe and even creative ways— that is, ways that help rekindle our lost energy for life. Anger can be released through therapeutic massage and through tears as readily as it can through shouting. In Chapter 10 I will discuss additional healthy, life-affirming ways to deal with strong emotion.

LINDA'S STORY

Linda took my grief class years after the death of her youngest child. Her story, which she wrote as part of the course work, was a painful one for me to read. In it, she candidly described her lifelong pattern of numbing herself in the face of her rage and helplessness. But she also inspired me when she described her courage in dealing with her repressed grief.

> When I was thirty-two the youngest of my seven children, three-and-a-half-year-old Janie, drowned while we were on a family vacation.
>
> My husband found her. She was in the water next to the pier. He tried to revive her while I called 911. But it was too late. She was pronounced dead on arrival. I don't remember sleeping for twenty-four hours. We just packed up our stuff and went back home.

[1]John W. Travis M.D., and Meryn G. Callander, *Wellness for Helping Professionals* (Mill Valley, CA: Wellness Associates Publications), 1990, p. E-11.

Telling my mother was probably the hardest thing I ever did. Then I realized I had six other children, that I couldn't fall apart for them. So I just shut down. Within forty-eight hours I denied my own grief with trance-like numbness and went headlong into taking care of my immediate and extended family as well as my friends. Their grief and pain were more important than mine. I allowed myself the luxury of grief only when I was alone or with someone not connected to me emotionally.

It was one more incident in a familiar pattern for me. When I experience a traumatic loss I enter a trance-like state, shut down my feelings with numbness, protect others' feelings, and take over. It took my child's death to start changing that pattern. But it took a long time.

When I was three years old I was the victim of incest by my paternal grandfather. During those violations I would become trance-like; my legs and feet would go numb.

When my grandfather died, my mother never dealt with her grief, anger, and fear, so I took it all on for her. She bore another child, a little girl, somebody to replace me in my dad's attention. My feeling of emotional abandonment at that time was crushing, but again I took on a trance-like numbness at this loss. My defenses were to take care of my mom's feelings and to take over in any other way I could to win back what I was losing.

By the time I was fourteen I was the oldest of nine children and had taken on the role of mother/wife. At sixteen I got pregnant and married. I did this with a trance-like numbness; it was my way out.

I now had someone else to take care of; I could act as if everything was okay. I was in control (or so I thought).

For twelve years after Janie's death my life was grey—I was in chronic low-grade depression. I was full of anger at God, but I couldn't express that. Instead, I blamed myself. For a time I thought that maybe I was being punished since we were Catholic but, contrary to Church teachings, we had decided that Janie was to be our last child.

Then seven years ago I got into therapy: grief counseling, recovery, and inner-child work. That's when I finally got to express my rage at God, my husband, my grandfather, myself. At last I was able to talk to my children about their sister's death in a real way. My children have gone through a lot, and they continue to. As their own children reach the age that Janie was when she died, I can see the fear in them, especially in being around water. It's amazing how much gets passed on from one generation to the next.

I had lost the ability to laugh. So many crises—it's no wonder. But now, after the grief work I've been doing, I am getting my spontaneity back. I'll actually catch myself laughing and say to myself "Where did that come from?" That laughter is telling me that I'm healing.

There is a lot I have accepted about Janie's death, but it is a pain that will never go away. I will continue to repeat the old pattern of numbing myself if I don't consciously experience the event over again. Most of the old patterns of reaction I used were necessary for my survival at the time. I didn't know what else to do or realize that I had other choices. But these patterns no longer work for me.

Things are different now. With the understanding that there is an ending, I am walking through my experiences with my eyes open, my feet on the ground, feeling my feelings, sharing with the significant others in my life, asking for support, taking care of myself.

A long time ago I used "reasons" to get me through the crisis. I told myself, "Janie is where I want all of us to be. . . ." Now that there is more acceptance, I don't know if I have a grasp of a reason. God's going to have to explain this one to me, and the reason had better be good! I'm sure there is growth in it, but I would rather have my child back and get the growth in another way.

I've accepted death as a fact of life, but I am not resigned.

IS IT ANGER OR SOMETHING ELSE?

Linda learned that releasing anger freed her to give attention to other aspects of her life that were "put on hold" temporarily. Coming face to face with strong emotion was highly instructive for her.

Anger can be instructive in another way, too. Many contemporary psychologists assert that anger is more often a warning signal—a "secondary emotion" that emerges to cover up a more primitive response less acceptable to the psyche.

My husband, Jere, gets angry, for example, whenever I happen to trip or hit my head on something (I am six foot three, so hitting my head is not uncommon). "Damn it," he might say. "What's wrong with you?" In the early years of our marriage this kind of blaming response was enough to send me into my own rage. "You asshole, I'm hurt and you're yelling at me for it?" But as we have worked together in uncovering the motivations behind many of our habitual responses, we have found that what Jere is really doing with his angry outburst is hiding his fear, inadequacy, and sadness. "If anything happens to hurt you," Jere has told me on several occasions, "I am immediately frightened. I start playing out scenarios of what I would do if you weren't around, and that brings on tremendous sadness. But I feel incompetent to be able to communicate my genuine caring for you. Instead, anger steps in, blaming steps in, and then I'm ashamed of myself for what I've done. Shame isn't easy to take, either, so I might become more angry just to cover that." We use similar strategies to cover up our feelings about children. The anger that many of us feel around the loss of a child or a relationship with a child is most likely a cover-up for some other feelings too painful to express.

It was that way in Lenora's case. Her grief over the handicaps of her two children expressed itself in raging against the teachers, the administration, the other children on the school bus. What she was feeling was intense fear and sadness, but anger became her outlet.

LENORA'S STORY

I lost the chance to be a normal mother of normal kids in a normal family when, just before kindergarten, my son was diagnosed as severely learning-disabled.

I knew nothing about learning disabilities. To me he looked and acted normal, but I was frustrated that he couldn't draw, didn't color, hated the water, wore shirts that were constantly dirty under his chin (because of drooling that I didn't notice—I just saw the dirty shirts), and spoke indistinctly. Other adults, some of them educators, assured me that he was fine, and that only added to the confusion.

Before that, I had blamed myself for the fact that he wasn't drawing or for other deficiencies. I figured it was because I was somehow lacking in mothering skills. So after the diagnosis I felt initial relief. At

least I knew something of what I was dealing with.
Many parents are dealing with problems that they
don't understand. It's hard to do your grief work if
you don't yet know what it is you're losing.

My own problems got bigger after that, though.
Parents of my son's friends didn't want him to play
with their perfect children, and after the first year the
schools fought me tooth and nail on delivering services. Some teachers thought we were overprotecting
him and refused to relate to his needs. My life was
filled with rejection, ostracism, confrontation, persis-
tence, fear, crises, concern, sadness.

Then my daughter, aged three, was diagnosed as an
insulin-dependent diabetic. The same social and
school problems occurred as with my son: Parents
didn't want my daughter playing with their children.
The school was afraid. I think the first-grade teacher
hated me even before she met me. The reactions of
people at large have been so grossly insensitive and
hurtful that I have a ball of RAGE inside me. I
remember that shortly after we moved into the new
neighborhood, one little "friend" of my daughter's
stood up on the bus and screamed to the other children that my daughter "can't have any sugar—that
one there!"

I constantly take my daughter to doctors. Last
month she needed to see a retinal specialist because
black spots had been seen on her retina. That is the
beginning of blindness, and she's only eleven. Two
years ago she had four seizures, and the two neurolo-
gists I consulted wanted her treated as an epileptic.
It was a horrible year. My constant fear and sadness
tear away at my sense of peace and happiness.

We don't fit in. What's easy for other families, like
an outing or a birthday party, for us requires intense

planning. I miss being carefree, being able to do many of the spontaneous, creative things with my children that other parents do with theirs. I miss being able to enjoy their participating in an activity. Instead, I'm always preparing for a problem.

We're very close, and I love my children tremendously, but when I stop and take a breath I have to admit that the pain of giving up my expectations and dealing with each new crisis has been tremendous, too.

I lost normality, an identity, carefreeness. I still mourn that. I would love to have a normal, easy, healthy, successful child. This has been and is so *hard*.

I am so sorry that my children have to endure pain beyond what I endure. Sometimes I wonder if they can bear it.

LENORA'S HEALING PROCESS

Having completed the writing of her story, Lenora reflected on what she had learned about the presence of anger in the process. She then went on to elaborate upon the steps she was taking in her healing.

As a result of writing about this loss, I became aware that sadness is underneath the rage I usually feel. The sadness is more primary, and it is very deep. This situation has affected me more pervasively than I had realized. Can I ever rid myself of the fear and anguish? I'm not sure I can, because new "horrors" keep presenting themselves. Sometimes I just feel overwhelmed by my fears.

A major priority for me is to take good care of myself. That's hard, though. I need to do things that others don't understand because they don't know how deep the anguish is and how constant a source of new anguish my situation is.

In many ways, I think we are a lot closer as a family because of what we've been through. I see that the children appreciate that, too. But then we've also always tried to give the children as much freedom as possible to work out their own lives. We've explained to them the consequences of what they'd have to deal with and then left them free to make their own decisions. When parents put too many restraints on their children, I think the kids become resentful.

Therapy has been necessary and helpful. I've also taken courses about grief and loss that have put things into perspective for me, too. I've started a parents' support group to work with others who are going through crises similar to mine.

Probably the greatest help of all has been that I've had several friends who call me regularly and ask me how things are going. I'm always amazed that people really seem to care. It is great to be able to ventilate my concerns and have someone listen and give regular feedback.

Overall, I've come to rely on a connection to something greater than myself. I've seen firsthand, in the eyes of the doctors who have worked with my children, that the medical profession can do only so much. There is a point at which no amount of intervention is going to help. Daily, I'm in a situation where I realize that there are other powers at work here that I can't control. I need to simply stay attuned to that.

Lately, I've begun to do some therapeutic bodywork and have begun to listen to and trust my own body more. It is telling me what it needs. I'm beginning to see that my mind was really an impediment to figuring things out. My dreams are helping, too.

In the final analysis, you must believe only in yourself, and in your child, and trust in the Higher Power.

All I can do, day by day, is keep doing my job. Some days that's really hard.

MOURNING THE LOSS OF A NORMAL LIFE

Like Lenora, those of us who have lost a child, or wanted a child and never had one, will mourn, with resentment, the loss of a "normal life." When one is grieving it does look as if everybody else has it easier and better. That may be true in some respects, but "normal" is another story.

Wherever we adopted the fantasy of "a normal life," "a normal family," and "normal children," that myth has persisted insidiously, has built a huge reservoir of discontent and anger, and for many of us has undermined the ability to enjoy life simply as it is, with all its joys and sorrows. If there is anything that needs to die it is this myth. We must tell the truth about it and then mourn it, the way we mourn the loss of Santa Claus or the idea of a utopia. Unless we do, we condemn ourselves to a life of intensified pain.

In all probability, the normality we are mourning is our own hungering for love. Since many of us never really felt as if we belonged here, never really bonded with our parents to the point where we learned to love and trust ourselves, we will continue to look for someone or something outside ourselves to satisfy this hunger. It's easier to build a fantasy of some normal life, and then mourn because we don't have it, than it is to deal with the primal condition—that is, the feeling that "I am not enough" and the constant confusion, ambivalence, and insecurity of our lives that follow from that assumption.

Grieving the losses related to children will bring up our expectations of normality in particularly poignant ways. Allowing ourselves to face and then dispel the fantasy of a perfect life offers us the chance to mourn what lives behind the fantasy: the fear of lack of love, the fear of our own lost innocence.

But even that, I have learned, is an illusion. Our innocence has never been lost, only obscured temporarily. At the heart of Being, love still lives. A tender spark, perhaps, but glowing.

DIFFERENT SPEEDS AND DIFFERENT STYLES

In all types of loss people will grieve at different "speeds." So sometimes one parent or family member is just finishing her grief and the other is just getting into it, just getting over the shock. Partners and family members tend to assume complementary roles at first: one member steps forward to handle details and often to caretake the other, who hangs back or withdraws. When the "strong one" plunges headlong into grief, the other may be more devastated, because now the script has changed. The situation escalates easily into one of extreme anger and confrontation, or degenerates into mutual isolation.

Knowing this, however, can encourage us to keep the lines of communication open throughout grief.

It is deadly to assume that, because your partner may not be expressing emotions in the same way you do, this means he or she is not feeling the emotion, even feeling it intensely. Women especially need to remember that men who are not expressive may still be feeling deeply. In fact, the man's pain is often greater simply because he feels that he must bear it without having adequate ways to show it.

In cases of separation or divorce I have heard one partner consistently angered and constantly lamenting: "It doesn't even seem to bother her (or him). She walks around with a smile on her face as if nothing is happening." We need to realize that the other person in the partnership is suffering as much as we are. Even when that is obvious to outside observers, the partners themselves often cannot see it. All one of the partners sees is the fact that the other seems able to take care of business while he or she feels completely lost and deep in suffering, or vice versa. Our grief and pain are frequently magnified by the projections of the mind.

One of the distinct advantages of using others for support is that we get some objective input about the place our projections are taking us.

Sometimes the stories of our losses have happy endings. Sometimes they don't. Sometimes the situation we have been grieving gets worse. That's when we need to remember that grieving is an ongoing process; that it is cyclic; that we may need to accept additional help, even if we've already "been through therapy" or done a lot of grieving before.

Michelle, who lost a relationship with her son because of his severe drug abuse, incarceration, and emotional withdrawal, mourned the loss with sadness, but her anger and outrage were always being re-ignited because of some new form of abuse on her son's part. The healing for Michelle is never complete. Her wound is always raw.

What will help Michelle will be essentially the same things that help others: an invitation and an opportunity to speak her story again. Her conversation with me was significant. It came at a time when she had for many months been feeling intense isolation.

> It felt so good to talk to you. It helped me clarify my feelings instead of just going over and over the same stuff in my head, where I get more muddled about it. It helped me affirm myself as a person. Most of all, I felt that it was okay that I had all these thoughts and feelings about my kids and about myself, even though they're not all "love and light." In fact, many of my

feelings are angry and resentful. It was wonderful to know that someone else could hear them and still care about me. Speaking again my affirmation that I must draw stronger boundaries with my son also helped me, and it reminded me of the need to get back into therapy again.

Michelle's story is one of ongoing brokenness, patching up, breaking again, moving on. And she is a survivor. She is using resources, she is working on herself, and she is being as honest as she can within her feelings as she journeys through her grief.

ANGER AND GRIEF AND THE HUMAN CONDITION

The loss of a child highlights the inadequacy of our language and our rituals to express the depth of human suffering. Where loss is concerned it is very difficult to "make nice." What can we say that will provide genuine consolation? What, if anything, can we say that will communicate adequately what it is we are feeling? Not much. More commonly, we will experience extreme discomfort and, if we are honest enough to admit it, even some resentfulness at the fact that this person's suffering is impinging on our lives. It's natural. For those of us who feel helpless or enraged at our own inability to communicate our needs, the faltering comments or euphemisms of others are a constant sore point.

Loss shines a laser beam on fleeting mortality—not just that of the children we have lost, but our own mortality as well. Every loss reminds us of every other loss in our lives, the past losses as well as those of the future. Since most people are exceedingly uncomfortable with death, that will reflect itself in the way they approach grief.

Every loss is a death of sorts. Every time you feel the sting of a lost opportunity, of having to give up your control, of having to admit that you don't know what to do next or that you were wrong, you "die" a little. But that doesn't have to be a negative experience. In fact, it can be a metaphor for a dynamic way of living. The "practice" of dying consciously can, in fact, keep one mindful of living life humbly and always remaining a beginner. Like the inhaling of air that fills the lungs and the exhaling of air that empties them, life and death are complementary parts of one ongoing process. Anything that reminds you of this continuity offers you a tiny chance to make your peace with the natural flow of life. Practicing that, your big losses, too, may be cast in a slightly different light.

These understandings are part of the core teaching of many great spiritual traditions. "Unless the grain of wheat dies it remains a grain of wheat, but when it dies it brings forth fruit in abundance," said the master Jesus (John 12:24). And the ancient philosopher Plato, instructing his students on his deathbed, was asked to summarize his life's work. According to legend he exhorted them to "practice dying."

FOR JOURNALLING

1. This first exercise is designed to help you specify the aspects of your loss you have accepted and the ones you are still unreconciled about. You can use this information to further explore your thoughts and feelings about your loss. As you reflect on these incomplete sentences, respond in as many ways as you care to.

   - With regard to my loss, I have accepted. . . .

• With regard to my loss, I cannot accept. . . .

Read back over what you have written. Now elaborate on each statement by writing some words of explanation or clarification or feeling. Do this by inserting the words *and* or *but* after each of your responses, and then continue the sentence as you wish. Here is one that I wrote a short time ago, for example: With regard to my loss, I have accepted that I will never bear children in my own body, and I want to always celebrate my womanhood in spite of that.

2. I pointed out in this chapter that different people grieve at different rates and with different styles. Use this exercise to explore some of the implications of those differences in your own case.
Your loss was undoubtedly "shared" by a member of the opposite sex, a partner, a friend, or another family member. And your judgment or understanding of his or her grief was probably different from your judgement or understanding of your own.

Write about your mate's or lover's or friend's responses during the time of your loss. What did you want from your partner or friend at the time? Was he or she capable of giving it? What do you want from him or her now?

3. Since any loss connects us with the ultimate loss— that is, death— this would be an advantageous time to write about your own death.

• What do you fear about death: pain, disability,

helplessness, dismemberment, the judgment of
God, the unknown, leaving family and friends,
the burden your death will be to others? Write
about any of these considerations.

- How did/do your parents deal with death?
- What questions do you have about death?
- If you have any children, how have you commu-
  nicated about death with them?

4. Summary: After completing any of these exercises, please write:
   "As a result of doing this work, I . . ." and finish the
   sentence in as many ways as you care to.

8

Is There a Right Choice?

You can't make the "right" decision.
You can only make the "best" deci-
sion.

MARTHA G.

I REMEMBER A definition I heard for the concept of tragedy," whispered Antonia, a young college-aged woman who was struggling with the decision of whether to have an abortion. She and I sipped tea in a secluded corner booth of an elegant restaurant. Antonia's hands played with the sugar bowl, lifting the lid, looking inside at the sugar cubes, closing the lid again, as we discussed tragedy. "It was a definition given to me in an eleventh grade literature class by Sister Josephine," Antonia continued, "that sweet old nun who looked as if she wouldn't know a tragedy if it stepped on her. 'Tragedy,' she drawled, 'is when two human beings look at the same situation, and each comes up with the opposite decision about the best thing to do.'" Antonia chuckled to herself, and then sighed, feeling again the weight of her thoughts. I was silent. Listening.

Antonia went on. "I never forgot that description. I guess that's why abortion is such a charged issue in this country. I guess that's part of the reason it's so hard for me to make a decision. I know I have those two human beings, with two opposing views, inside me all the time."

Antonia made her decision within a few days of our visit together. She had an abortion. But, like so many of the millions of woman who make that same decision every year, it was not without a time of excruciating self-questioning, one that carried with it a good deal of emotional pain.

I know that not everyone who has an abortion appears to suffer later; many remain grateful that they were able to make what for them was the right decision and feel glad that they made it. But into my classes have come those for whom the decision was an excruciating one and for whom the termination of the pregnancy remained an emotional problem for years to come.

Antonia, for example, as a student in my course in Holistic Health, two years after her abortion drew a life-sized portrait of her body as part of an assignment in self-awareness. While the major part of the body was colored in pastels and decorated with beautiful and positive symbols, the lower trunk was dark. Antonia had surrounded her womb and vagina with grey tones.

She was still in mourning.

My purpose in this book is not to address the ethics of abortion or any other child-related loss. Beyond any question of right or wrong I am concerned only with every person's need to grieve her or his lost children, born or unborn. It is my belief that only in the grieving will it be possible to accept, and thus integrate, the choices we have made.

Decisions, choices, preferences: these are buzzwords in our society. Popularly, they are synonymous with freedom and independence. Unlike those who live under totalitarian regimes, we can vote for many different candidates. We can choose any religion, any form of education, any soap powder, or any brand of jeans we can afford. Our freedom to make choices and to cater to our preferences is often heralded as a sign of our advanced civilization. But when those choices involve having surgery or not, becoming pregnant or not, terminating a pregnancy or not, adopting or not, remaining child-free or not, placing one's child for adoption or not, securing joint custody or not, instituting life-support systems and extraordinary measures or not, resorting to artificial insemination or not, engaging in legal battles or not . . . freedom may seem "like a rip-off," as one man put it. The multiplicity of our choices, the ethical implications of our choices, and the knowledge that we must live with the consequences of our choices—these are the issues that may freeze us with fear, haunt us, tire us out. "I just wanted somebody else to tell me the right thing to do," said Dana, as she contemplated a risky surgery as a way to deal with her infertility. "But, of course, my doctor wouldn't and couldn't do that." Our choices must be our own.

Regardless of race, religion, or state of health, the woman who must make a decision regarding a child in her life may labor through an internal labyrinth and, at the same time, feel exploited, shamed, possibly condemned for being a less-than-perfect mother or an inadequate provider. She may be looked at as being indulgent and selfish if she decides to remain child-free or realizes that someone else can raise her child better than she can. She will often feel damned if she does and damned if she doesn't.

Women's partners go through similar tribulations and have similar feelings about those choices. They know that such a decision will irrevocably affect not only the rest of *their* lives but the entire life of the child.

They must make their decisions on the basis of an assessment of their circumstances at the time—a clear, altruistic assessment; perhaps a fear-filled, selfish assessment; a heroic, heartbreaking, or relief-giving assessment. They make the decision based on what they feel capable of doing at the time. They make the best decision they can, all things considered, at the time!

A fifty-two-year-old woman named Angela, whom I've worked with for several years, spoke compassionately about the dilemma she faced more than twenty-five years ago in deciding what was best for her child.

> I know I did the best I could under the circumstances. I knew then that I couldn't take care of this baby and that the father would not be appropriate, either. There was at that time a great stigma on an unwed mother. I knew I would have to give her up. I knew I wanted to give the child the very best that I could.

DANA'S STORY

As a member of an organization for couples learning to deal with infertility, Dana, a professional woman in her mid-thirties, speaks for many hopeful parents in describing the terror and frustration of decision-making.

> For me, becoming pregnant the first time involved a full year of tests, and then taking infertility drugs. For others, it means starting one procedure, letting it go for a while, and then, when it doesn't work, moving on to something else.
>
> Treatments have to be timed. There are so many details, so many decisions—about surgeries, about risk factors, about adoption. You can easily feel over-whelmed.

At some point you get disgusted. Or you might become assertive and activist in your approach, trying to learn all you can about infertility and the options. General practitioners and even OB-GYNS can't always give you the answers you want, but few will admit they don't know. That makes it more difficult.

Once you find a specialist who deals with infertility, that specialist is not usually intimidated by people with knowledge of their condition. The specialist will plot a course of action so that you feel you're progressing, but at the same time, he or she will not tell you when "enough is enough." The specialist wants you to have a child, and quite often there is no medical reason for your not becoming pregnant. So you keep trying. The plan designed for you will keep going until you say you want to stop completely.

This decision to stop trying is a big problem in infertility. It can create a lot of stress and complications. Almost always, some new form of technology or treatment appears that just might work in your case. I know of people who have had seven or eight miscarriages and as many different surgeries.

Once you finally get to feel that things are happening, just to have a doctor say "This operation will increase your chances by fifty percent" makes it easy to get caught up in the enthusiasm of the moment.

For some people the point of surgery is the point at which they draw the line. I took drugs to shrink my fibroids, and they helped. But sometimes you end up taking so many drugs that you don't even know who you are any more; they all alter your mood. You get focused on having the baby, you read everything and try everything, and in the meantime your body is swimming in drugs, and you hope that the long-term effects are not going to be harmful.

Your relationship to sex changes dramatically, too. Everything revolves around your ovulation. Your phases become all-important. You don't necessarily feel like having sex, neither does he. He starts to feel like a stud service. "We have to do it—today, tomorrow, and Friday," you tell him. And you'd better not be out of town on that day, or decide to go camping. The process changes your life. When you've spent $300 a month on fertility drugs you do not want to miss that one chance each month to become pregnant.

Emotionally, some women go through changes in self-image during their treatments for infertility. It's even harder in some ways for infertile men: they tend to equate infertility with impotence. Women who described themselves positively before the treatment begin, once the treatment is underway, to use words like "fat," "dysfunctional," "ugly" and "empty."

Then comes a miscarriage, and it's all over. The terrible "M" word. It's a terrible moment, akin to a death. No one really knows how much you hurt. When I had one, my husband internalized it more. He kept busy. He felt worse for me. I was a bit upset that he wasn't reacting more. He was more analytical, as if this would never have happened anyway. After trying so hard, having it slip through your fingers makes the loss so much harder. You lose confidence.

Even your parents frequently don't understand. "No one else in our family has this problem." Thanks, Mom. So I'm left feeling like the mutant. I was somewhat estranged from my parents after my mother said that—and a little more aloof. She made no effort to find out anything about what I was going through. To her, the miscarriage was "so what?" Even people who do have children say amazingly insensitive things: "Oh, children are difficult." Or "It's for the best."

As with all grief, just when you think you're over it, it comes flooding back. In the supermarket shortly after my miscarriage, I saw a pregnant woman and a woman with a new baby. I just almost lost it. I had to fight to avoid breaking down into hysterical sobbing.

Once the miscarriage is over, immediately the future looms: "What are we going to do now? Are we going to have to go through it all over again?" It's not only the drugs that make it difficult; the emotional process is so taxing. Now there are a whole new series of decisions to make.

The biggest source of help was to have someone else to speak with. Listening to other people's stories is consoling and humbling. It is so important to talk to other people who have gone through what you are just in the middle of. RESOLVE was beneficial for me; it's an organization that gives referrals and support and information about medical alternatives, adoptions, and child-free living to individuals and couples experiencing infertility. You don't have to go through this alone.

Honestly, the adversity of our infertility treatments brought my husband and me closer together. We have a daughter now, but the days of darkness do not simply fade away, they left an indelible smudge on my life. Now we contemplate the next set of decisions—are we ready or willing to go through this process all over again to have another child? At a recent party, a young woman who saw me with my daughter asked if she could rub against me. She was planning to get pregnant next year and wanted a girl. My bittersweet smile confused her. "It's a private joke," I said.

DOUBTS AND CHOICES

Even after you have made a firm decision about your child-related loss, you will still cycle through periods of doubt. You will still have to mourn some aspects of your choice even if you feel completely at peace about it. Because of the strength required to make certain decisions, you might for a time push your grief away, knowing that going into it will take a lot of energy, energy that you do not currently have. That's okay. Simply be prepared for grieving to show up in unexpected ways. It might be overpowering: a memory that rouses you from sleep, or a vivid dream in which you give birth to a child and raise it. For others it may be a fleeting reflection as they pass the hospital where a procedure was enacted, or a tug at the heart and a second glance when they pass a young man in the street who has the same hair coloring as their child had and looks to be about the same age. Some will cry. Some will rage. Some will merely remember, mourning a loss quietly every year when their child's "birthday" rolls around. Grief can show up at the time of the decision, soon after, or not until years later. In my own case grief becomes more poignant as I get older.

Nearly a year after her abortion, Jeanette, a nineteen-year-old student of mine, wrote of her lost child, "I thought somehow your spirit would melt away within your distorted body, that you'd vanish from my life as soon as they cut you off. Eleven months later, and you've found me. You follow me around dragging your doll by its legs, asking for forgiveness."

The initial experience of grief or its sudden reappearance may challenge your conviction about the decision. Commonly, people mistake necessary grief for some sort of indication that they have made a mistake in their decision. That isn't true.

For others, later circumstances may cause pain, self-doubt, and regret over earlier decisions. The woman who finds herself unable to conceive at thirty-two will be confronted by memories of her decision to have an abortion when she was twenty-one. The couple who has postponed childbearing until the time was "right" may find that it is too late. People in these situations frequently blame themselves or feel that they are being punished, even though they know better rationally. Support groups can help at times like this. It is essential to remember that hindsight is always twenty-twenty. Your decision might have been different then, if you had known. Perhaps. The point is, you didn't, and couldn't.

For Margaret, fifteen years after her abortion, there are still vestiges of grief. Rather than denying her pain, however, Margaret has turned to face her soul-searching questions about the social implications of abortion.

MARGARET'S STORY

At the time of choosing to have an abortion I remember feeling how important it was to have the right to make that choice. And, fortunately for me, abortion was legal in my city. The women's clinic was a very elegant and modern place, and I went through the whole procedure quite easily. But what I had not been prepared for were the ramifications of making that choice, ramifications that I have only now—fifteen years later—begun to consider. It's not really an issue for me from a moral right-and-wrong perspective. It's not black-and-white.

Families in India today are choosing sex-select abortions (aborting only female fetuses) with the rationale: "Why can't I have what I want?" "Why shouldn't I have a choice between a boy and a girl?" The real reason is that sons are considered desirable in that culture, and daughters are costly—they require a dowry when they marry, and the poor, especially, can't afford that.

My growing question is, "What does this have to say about our need to evolve into real responsibility?" I feel caught, as so many women do, because I believe it's oppressive to rob a woman of a legal choice. But to have a government make any rules either way is dangerous, because each case is uniquely circumstantial. Often, only someone who has for quite some time known and loved the woman involved might be able to evaluate what would serve her best. That person could help the woman who is pregnant come to the most mature decision.

This question seems like a nightmare to me. I don't see an easy answer, and that causes me a lot of pain.

WHO SAYS "NO"?

Massive numbers of men and women born between 1946 and 1955, the "baby-boomer" years, aren't having babies. In fact, compared to their mothers' generation, the female baby-boomers are twice as likely not to have children. One in five women of this age group is without children, and the rate increases to one in four among college-educated women.

While some people choose to have a child to heal the wound of their own childhood, others choose the opposite. Bringing a child into the world, exposing a helpless infant to a degree of suffering similar to that which we ourselves went through, may be too terrible to think about. "At the time of my sterilization," commented Ella, a forty-year-old artist who at the age of twenty-eight chose a tubal ligation, "I was convinced that the world was in such a sorry state that children should not be subjected to it." Another woman described her choice as one based on "positive moral values . . . since an American born into the world puts unconscionable pressures on natural resources."

Or a woman may simply feel no attraction to the idea of having children in her life and choose to forego that experience in favor of pursuing her career. As one university professor put it, "I chose to live with adults, working with young people who are more mature."

For some, there is a clear sense of purpose, a peace about their choice, even if it was a choice made by default. Even so, probing a little deeper, I have found that pain is often associated with that decision. For Janice, today a brilliant accountant in a large firm, children were a "nuisance," a condition she had borne throughout her own teenage years as the eldest daughter in a large family. For Rita, whose mother had continually told her she was a stupid child while showering attention on Rita's younger sister, children were feared. For Ruth, children would require something that she felt she wasn't capable of supplying: a sense of responsibility that she wasn't prepared to shoulder. That hurt, even though she was reconciled to her decision and felt strong about it.

"Making a decision about children has one curious aspect," Ingrid told me. She was forty-nine at the time of our interview and just beginning to feel the implications of her decision.

> I always held out to myself the idea that I could change it, and of course I could have. But time goes by very quickly, and now it is simply too late. I never realized that my postponement was really a lifetime decision. Not until recently. I consequently never recognized the grief surrounding it.
>
> Even though I feel good about my choice and I would make the same decision again, there is still some grieving to do. I mourn something that I never had. I think mothers mourn the loss of their independence, but I think some of us need to face the fact that we need to mourn not having someone dependent on us.

Sometimes it is a woman's mate who has made the choice not to have children. He may have had a vasectomy early in his life, or opted for it in a previous marriage. "When we first started going together," whispered Jan, looking a bit ashamed, "he told me that he didn't want kids and asked me not to try to change his mind. It was just something we never discussed after that." Some men are unwilling or unable to bear the responsibility for more, or any, children. And their reasons are as many as the individuals questioned, but their wounds are evident nonetheless when they dare to speak about their own childhood traumas. A handsome young man in his mid-twenties who had already fathered three children by three different mates, Jessie lived with none of them and claimed he didn't want to. His own youth had been dominated by a smothering mother who rarely let him away from her side. "I guess maybe I'm getting back at her in some way," he reflected, contorting his face as he spoke about "Mom."

The condition of being child-free is not, of course, always voluntary. A physical condition may create infertility in either a man or a woman; a hysterectomy, or the warning that to bear a child would mean a serious impairment of the woman's health, can for many couples level the gavel on freedom of choice. Certainly, the option is always open to choose a child-free state or to adopt a child, but for many people that option is neither thought to be desirable nor pursued as possible. For those couples, or singles, who do adopt a child or reconcile to their child-free lifestyle, that act in and of itself may not obviate the need to grieve the loss of one's own physical capacity for mothering or fathering.

Some individuals want a child desperately but only as the outcome of a bonded relationship with a member of the opposite sex. When life circumstances are such that they never find a suitable match, never marry, or divorce before children are conceived, the longing for a child will not be easily diminished. "If only I were younger, I am sure I would have a baby, no matter what," wrote a fifty-two-year-old single woman.

Society's norms make bearing or raising children a hard if not impossible choice for many people. A woman without a mate who chooses to have a child on her own faces a hard road. The lesbian or gay couple, even if they both want children, must consider the additional social stigma, both for themselves and for their child, that such a decision may entail. A single man who loves children but doesn't wish to marry faces legal restrictions and social expectations that may be insurmountable. The wound of childlessness that some experience is therefore, at least in part, a cultural wound.

In the case of individuals who relinquish their right to parenthood as an aspect of religious dedication—as with celibate nuns and priests, or those who hold a vision for world service that leaves them without a personal life—they often assume too readily that the grace of the "calling" compensates for the sacrifice. And for some, it does. For those rare individuals who are able to sublimate the sex drive or "mothering" or "fathering" instinct into a life of service, the choice is one that leads to tremendous spiritual enrichment.

Too many, however, took the vow of celibacy without ever honestly grieving the consequences. They attempted a spiritual "by-pass," a premature heroism that showed its effects only in later years. High rates of alcoholism stalk the ranks of the clergy. A disproportionately high percentage of uterine cancer is prevalent among nuns, a connection that I view, from my own experience, as indicative of some imbalanced relationship to sexuality. In the past twenty years large numbers of nuns and priests, acknowledging the loss of their idealism, have left the monastic life for marriage and parenthood, some after thirty or more years of celibacy. Others have opted for a dual life, carrying on clandestine sexual relationships, and even bearing children, while still holding on to the security and prestige of "religious" life.

HOW WE DEAL WITH OUR DECISIONS

The stages we go through in grief as outlined by Elisabeth Kubler-Ross have guided educators and therapists in giving the public a framework on which to hang its pain, confusion, and outrage at the necessary losses that comprise the stuff of our lives.

As I talked with my students and friends about the difficult decisions they were called to make regarding child-related loss, I found their responses tended to fall quite naturally into one of the stages specified by Kubler-Ross. The first stage is denial. With some people I observed this denial in their firm conviction that they felt nothing. "There was no decision to be made," they might say. "I never wanted kids in the first place." Others disclosed making fantastic promises that they knew they would never keep, a subtle form of denial through postponement. "If I ever got my money-trip together I would adopt a child," wrote one older woman who lived alone. "Someday, when I feel more emotionally stable . . ." went some stories.

Anger, another stage of grieving, was often associated with the decision or with its consequences. One woman expressed that anger toward herself, judging her life a failure. "I often feel as if there must be something seriously wrong with me for not being able to maintain a partnership for any length of time," she told me.

Another woman, in commenting about her many surgeries during infertility treatment, wrote:

> I never got any support to stop (the treatments). Now that I have stopped, I find this (my decision) shocking. How will you know when you've gone too far—or, even better, far enough? I wish I could tell you. I know the point is different for everyone. You can go too far, and there can be a serious price to pay. Intuition should tell us that you can't have surgery performed on your reproductive organs seven times

without having some kind of major impact. I am experiencing terrible anger about the fact that I didn't take care of myself and that those that love me didn't take care of me, either.[1]

Sadness or pining about the consequences of the decision is a stage in the grieving process, and many women and men will disclose that they often feel a physical pain when they see a family interacting happily together. For Joyce, holidays and family reunions were painful times. "All my brothers and sisters have children, and of course they get the attention at these family affairs. I feel as if I have to be really productive in other ways to convince my parents that maybe I've contributed something to society besides kids."

Ed, whose wife had a necessary hysterectomy early in their marriage, told me, "The look that kids give to their Dads, that look of total trust, admiration, even idolization—when I see that I get a twinge. I feel sad then that I never really had much of a choice about having children." Like so many others, Ed resigned himself to a "childless" life, rationalizing the situation as a sign from God or a turn of fate. "If we are ever meant to adopt children, I guess God will give us another sign," he confessed. His rationalizations were easily interpreted as acceptance. But further conversation revealed that this relaxed, "take-what-comes" attitude was based on a deep feeling of unworthiness—the sense that he had no right to make any willful decision for himself, let alone make any legitimate requests of life or God. It took gentle, slow work on Ed's part, and supportive encouragement from his wife, who was well along in her own grieving process, to invite him to look more closely at his loss.

---

[1]Jeanne Sedgwick, "Support to Stop," *RESOLVE Newsletter of Northern California*, February-March 1992.

Women are built for childbearing, and men are built for child-making, and even with the intellectual or spiritual resolution we may have made about not wanting or needing children, there is often some residue of grief left—some reason behind this choice or attitude that may never have been faced squarely, no less mourned. That unmourned reason, like every type of unmourned loss, can take its toll in the body—as it did in my case—or in the psyche, as a form of self-hatred or self-doubt. As we tell our stories and write the painful questions in our hearts, we reveal these reasons, we embrace them, we grow stronger in living with the pain, and we even come to celebrate the hand of God in closing one door as we open another.

DIANE'S STORY

Diane was enthusiastic as she told us her story. Her decision to carry her child to full term and then to place him for adoption was not easily made, but the whole experience marked a necessary milestone in her growth and development into maturity. She shared with us the conviction that she sincerely celebrated her choices.

> Not every woman has a devastating time with having a child and giving it up. It seems that our lack of clear rites of passage from childhood to adult life leaves us in a void of meaningful expression and validation of our step into maturity. A situation of having a child, even if one has grief with that decision, is always a rite of passage. And I consider that to be one of the biggest gifts I ever gave myself. The decision to give up my child for adoption necessitated a step into maturity and responsibility that I hadn't been willing to take on so fully before. Sure, it wounds us, but it seasons us, too.

Diane's story held many of the responses typical to an

unplanned pregnancy: the denial, the increased tension with her lover, the surprise at finally realizing she was pregnant. She had complicated the situation by moving out on her own and determining that she was going to work to support herself throughout the pregnancy. She took a job as a mother's helper.

> The first woman I worked for was blatantly cruel. At one point she said to me, "I think it's good that my children see how miserable you are so that they will never do what you have done." I lasted at this place for a few weeks and then moved on to another home. The woman here seemed kinder, at first, but as time went on it was evident what a selfish and stingy person she was. I was eight months pregnant and I was always hungry, and she was literally rationing my food for me.
>
> No matter how bad it got, though, I realized that I was the "home" for the baby I was carrying, that everything about me was what the child was getting. And I knew I wanted to give the child the very best that I could. For me that meant no self-pity, no craziness. I knew I needed to stay as healthy and strong as possible, both inside and out. I was not projecting sorrow, longing, or pain. I was projecting love. It was real. It wasn't suppression. I knew that is what needed to be done. So I did it.
>
> The whole experience was a positive and growing one, despite the pain I had to endure throughout. I know I did the best under the circumstances, and watching my child being born was ecstatic.
>
> The adoption agency had asked me if I would like to feed the baby after its birth. At first I said "No," but in thinking of it I decided I would do it. I fed the child three times a day for those three days. I had to hold my resolve. I fed the child from a bottle rather than from the breast. Feeding him was a wonderful, warm,

fulfilling experience. I felt I communicated my love
for him and that I wasn't giving him up for the lack of
it. At first he wasn't eating very well, but that
improved over the several days I fed him. It was
cleansing and a completion for us, and very peaceful.

An outcome was that my body felt more opened
and womanly during and after the pregnancy. I felt
that I could move. I had lost some rigidity. I am so
grateful to have had a baby, to have chosen to feed
him, to have experienced the closeness and the successful transference of love from my body to his. I'm
certain he came from being loved and wanted, not
unloved and unwanted.

Diane reached for a tissue out of the box near her chair,
and I noticed that she was trying to hold back her tears.
Even though she had handled this important piece of her life
with self-assurance, there were vestiges of it that, after
telling her story, were only now being mourned.

"Go ahead, Diane," I gently encouraged her. "There's
more to say, yes?"

Her face contorted for an instant before the tears
began. "Today I miss the fact that this nurturing experience
was not of longer duration, and that I didn't have the experience of bringing up a child," she continued, sobbing softly. "I
am sorry that I gave him his father's name, which makes him
less traceable for me. He can't trace me that way, either, if
he should want to. I wish now that I could adopt a baby. If
only it were possible, I would do it."

Susan and I were silent for a long time after that.
Diane seemed disturbed by her breakdown, and, after a few
minutes, I spoke to her. I told her about my own experience
of finding that even a situation we now hold as essentially
positive can still ignite blazes from other aspects of our lives
where we have not yet fully grieved. Diane was approaching

menopause and consequently facing the loss of her potential as a child-bearer. Her memories were pushing her ahead into the next developmental phase of this life of loss.

It is important to realize that because we still cry about our losses, that does not mean that we haven't done the grief work necessary for recovery. We will carry these wounds forever, and we will grow from them, but they will still hurt no matter how many years have passed. We can recall the famous poem by Robert Frost:

> *I shall be telling this with a sigh*
> *Somewhere ages and ages hence:*
> *Two roads diverged in a wood, and I—*
> *I took the one less traveled by,*
> *And that has made all the difference.*

MAKING THE BEST DECISIONS

Decisions are rarely easy or clear-cut, but you can maximize your chances of making the best decision in the moment by keeping a few simple thoughts in mind.

First: Don't let yourself succumb to the pressure of having to make any decision on the spot. Of course, where there is a medical emergency, that may not always be possible, but usually, even if surgery is the option suggested to you, there is time to consider it. Surgeons, like other professionals, are busy people. They want to be able to plan their schedules to suit their other priorities. Don't let that discourage you from asserting your right to take the time you need to "sit with" your question.

Second: Get several opinions, especially where medical issues are concerned. Read the literature. Talk to other people who have gone through similar experiences. Become an informed consumer. It is easy to feel discouraged and to want this painful decision to simply "go away," and that might encourage you to follow the first path you come to. Wait. Take a long look at it. Explore the other paths.

Third: Use support groups, clergy, therapists, or friends, especially those who have some background in these issues. Talk to them. Ask them how they made their decisions. Let them support you in your ambivalence and confusion and help remind you that your feelings are normal in the process of grief.

Fourth: Avoid adding additional stress to yourself by taking on any other big life changes during this time. Don't move to a new house. Don't change jobs or take on any new financial responsibilities if you can possibly help it. Support yourself by keeping some regularity and predictability in other aspects of your life.

Fifth: Use prayer, meditation, God, or a connection to a Higher Power. Ask for the strength and clarity to see what is most beneficial to you at this time. Realize that all decisions are made on the basis of incomplete information, and ask for the faith and trust to be able to live with whatever decision you make.

Sixth: Use the exercises listed below for journalling about your decisions and your loss.

FOR JOURNALLING

Writing can help you at the three stages of making your decision. Before you make it, writing will allow you to explore your options on paper. When you are coming to a decision, it will give you an outlet for your feelings. Afterward, writing can be a way to assure you that you made the best decision possible at the time.

Before your decision: We all have "parts" of ourselves that are frequently in conflict about our decisions. The practical "part" says one thing. The altruistic "part" says another. The voice of our internalized "parent" may say something else. It is sometimes helpful to give voice to as many of these parts as possible.

Allow each voice to plead her case fully by writing it out, without judgment or interruption from the others. Read back over all the cases. Ask the voice that represents compassion and ultimate wisdom to write a few words of summary.

While coming to a decision: We all have different approaches to decision-making, but most of us follow a pattern in the way we approach decisions that is similar to the way we approach conflict. Some of us procrastinate. Some of us will never let ourselves be satisfied with completion. Some of us run away. Some of us are perfectionistic. Learning to identify your pattern in handling conflicts can give you some additional information that can help you understand the strong or strange emotions or physical reactions you may be having now. To help you identify your own pattern, complete the following sentences:

During times of transition or times of conflict I. . . .

When faced with difficult decisions I. . . .

What would make this whole process easier would be. . . .

After your decision: Write a long letter to yourself explaining the difficulties you are still having in weighing all the factors in your case. Hold on to this letter for the future and read it whenever you have doubts that you may have done "the right thing."

After performing any of these exercises, bring closure to your writing by completing the following sentence in as many ways as you care to:

As a result of doing this writing I. . . .

9

Something to Live for, Again

THE NAVAJO, the Taoist, and the Zen Buddhist traditions each have a similar saying about the way life unfolds. Loosely rendered, the saying goes: Beautiful in the beginning; beautiful in the middle; beautiful in the end. It reflects the transitory nature of existence, as it also invites one to bring attention and care to every phase of every activity.

In grief work this attitude applies on many levels. First, it is encouraging to know that just as the process of grief has a beginning and a middle, so too has it an end. Healing *does* happen, sometimes in spite of us. Things don't just fall apart and stay apart. Life reorganizes itself, oftentimes on a higher, more conscious, more compassionate level.

Second, this statement reminds us that our endings are no *more* important, and certainly no *less* important, than our beginnings. While we may devote a lot of energy to working through our grief when we are in the midst of our most acute pain, this saying reminds us that we ought to be as observant and open to help in the ending phases as we were earlier. Our endings are the beginnings of the next stage in our evolution.

Third, saying that all things are "beautiful" in the beginning, the middle, and the end does not imply that all things are "pretty" or "happy" or "painless" or anything like that. *Beautiful* here means something objective. More precisely, it translates as "harmonious," in the sense that all things have their proper place in creation, whether that place is one of inspiring us with happiness or causing us to weep in sadness. All things are just what they are. And all things are good.

Whether or not you can subscribe entirely to such a philosophy will be a matter of personal choice. Nevertheless, in this chapter I will be underscoring the powerful human capacity (perhaps even a natural tendency) for using our adversity as a springboard for something akin to love. For me, that's "beautiful." And I heard this sentiment echoed, or at least implied, in every story and interview I conducted for this book.

This chapter will be an invitation to keep perspective. It will at least urge you to remember your strengths and resources as you experience your helplessness and weakness and mourn your losses. At best, it will hint at the possibility of transformation through the alchemical fire of suffering.

None of this is meant to force your grieving process to move any faster than it is. It's not a question of speed. It's a question of balance.

LIFE IN THE NEUTRAL ZONE

In his book, *Transitions: Making Sense of Life's Changes,* author Bill Bridges divides the cycle of change (which is synonymous with the cycle of grief) into three stages: the endings, the neutral zone, and the beginnings. In using this book with my students in grief education, I find that his reversal of the order of elements in the cycle provides a potent metaphor that almost everyone can relate to. Furthermore, the concept of the neutral zone offers tremendous consolation and encouragement.

For Bridges, the neutral zone refers to the time between "death" (an ending or loss of any kind) and "rebirth" (our initiation into the next phase of life). It is a time in which stalling is common. We are adjusting, slowly, to our losses, but are unsure of what comes next. We are waiting—another characteristic of both the neutral zone and the feminine approach to existence. It may be a time of doing nothing in particular, having little motivation, not being able to figure things out at the logical level, even though the "mind in the body" may be amazingly diligent. It is a time for watching our dreams for what they have to say, a time when the unconscious is at work more strongly. It is a time to explore, with whatever means are available, the notion of surrender.

Knowing that "neutral zones" are part of the process, we no longer have to berate ourselves for our indecisiveness or ambivalence. We can and should, in fact, prize them.

The neutral zone is inherently a spacious place—a place to knock around in while we recuperate. Our willingness to cultivate the practice of "internal spaciousness" will be a great asset in furthering our healing. If we tense up around pain, we will increase it. As we relax, pain tends to lessen. This goes for emotional as well as physical pain.

Steven Levine, who has written several books on grief and loss and has worked with thousands of dying people and their families, speaks about "bringing loving kindness" rather than the usual self-hatred and constriction to our pain. Loving kindness, or spaciousness, provides us with a little breathing space in which to contemplate, or prepare for the next wave. The neutral zone is full of breathing space.

Susan, in the healing process following her miscarriage,

characterized her neutral zone as a time of disappointment. Diving into that particular wave for as long as was necessary, she eventually surfaced with heightened sensitivity and renewed compassion both for herself and others. For Susan, the neutral zone was a time of remembering, of allowing tears, and a time of integrating her loss into the framework of her spiritual practice. The neutral zone was a time of preparation for healing, a time still shadowed with pain but occasionally illuminated with a ray of hope. Susan spoke of her healing in these paradoxical terms:

SUSAN'S HEALING

My partner gave me a gift when he named and gave me permission to feel disappointment—a word that I found had profound meaning for me, a word that was different from sorrow or pain or grief. It was "my word"—the one that touched with such a tender hand that it never failed to break through my testy, short-tempered mood and draw from me the tears that were waiting so close beneath the surface of my anger, the tears that were accomplishing my healing.

"I think I'm still really upset about losing the baby," I would say in response to his questions about what was bothering me at any particular time.

"It's natural to be disappointed," he would gently assure me, again, and again, and again.

Allowing disappointment to unfold inside me, petal by petal, or to flow over me, stream after stream, wore down the tensions I had been holding, tensions that were just temporary, protective shields against the thing I most needed and wanted to do: to grieve in order that I would heal and grow to accept.

Disappointment is a particularly delicate texture of loss. It arises when our desired outcome for something doesn't happen or is less than we expected. And how ripe we are for that kind of "expecting" when we are carrying, or hoping for, a child. In fact, that is the word commonly used to describe pregnancy. "They're expecting," people will say. And in my own case I found that almost immediately after I discovered I was pregnant there were many moments in which I already held the baby in my arms, or watched my child of five run across the yard or my fifteen-year-old coming home from school. No wonder I was disappointed. I had already accomplished my future through my own imagination.

It's natural to imagine. But it can be dangerous, too, if we neglect the here-and-now—the only place where genuine satisfaction is found. I believe I saved myself a lot of unnecessary pain with the second miscarriage because, with the blessed wisdom of experience, I consciously refrained from getting carried away by my dreams of the future. Instead, I told myself to take it one day at a time.

It was healthy to avoid fantasies of the future, yet it was tricky not to fall into fatalism—that is, to avoid accepting the pregnancy just in case it didn't work out. Seeing how often I used that attitude of fatalism early in my pregnancy, I was horrified to think that I might pass on that strategy for coping with life to my own child. It was simply too high a price to pay.

So I had asked my mate and friends to remind me of my vow to be different this time, and I began to practice accepting and loving this new presence in my body without drawing any conclusions for the future.

For me, remembering to live in the present moment and allowing myself to feel disappointment without fatalism is actually a "practice"—something that must be worked at, day in and day out, the way one builds up muscles before a big race.

Remembering my practice often brought about a
spontaneous change as my fears relaxed. As long as I
didn't become compulsive or perfectionistic about my
practice, but approached my old habits with gentleness, compassion, and even a sense of humor, I felt
great strength in being different.

This principle of working with the fantasy-produc-
ing mind was clearly expressed in an interview with
the Dalai Lama, the spiritual and temporal ruler of
Tibet, and a celibate monk. The interviewer asked
the Dalai Lama if he ever thinks of beautiful women
or is tempted by beautiful women. With child-like can-
dor the Tibetan lama admitted that he did think of
beautiful women, that in fact he sometimes dreamed
of them. Yet even in his dreams he would practice his
life-long discipline, reminding himself that "I am
monk." He concluded by explaining that in fact, he
never thinks of himself as the Dalai Lama, but only as
a simple monk. Reading that, I thought to myself,
"Now, that is why *he* is the Dalai Lama," and I was
greatly relieved. If even the Dalai Lama, raised in a
religious culture and chosen for his position as a
young child, has to continually remind himself that *he*
is a monk, then surely there is no reason to feel self-
critical or guilty when I forget my purposes.

Pain often discourages relationship. When we are
in it we realize how deeply alone we are. Our loss is
ours, and no one else can endure it for us. And that
recognition tends to harden us into a stance of brav-
ery, or independence, or self-pity, or helplessness.
But each time I was reminded that disappointment
was natural, whether I was lashing out at friends or
simply carrying on in my workaday world with a
closed and hurting heart, that remembrance would
trigger my tears. And when the tears came, plunging

me to the heart of being disappointed, I was vulnerable and open again. Suddenly there was space for people to approach me and be affectionate—to just hold me or rock me, or cry with me.

When my partner said "I am so disappointed, too," I really heard him. I was shocked to realize that I had guarded myself against hearing his grief, for fear that it would increase mine. Yet the opposite was true. By acknowledging that my mate and my close friends were really sad, too, that it was a grieving that we shared, I was finally able to give something to them from beyond the locked-in place of my own suffering. This change was a real blessing.

For me, disappointment touches closer to the heart of grief than anger does. I don't want to underestimate the value and necessity of our stronger emotions, like anger, but I think it is common that I can cheat myself by stopping there, or by indulging these emotional states past the point of their immediate value. Here, again, is another slippery ledge to navigate. How I find that point of distinction between anger-well-placed and anger-indulged is a matter of experience. At first I had to give myself permission to play out the anger of the two-year-old child, who becomes infuriated to learn that she is not the center of the universe or that life just isn't fair.

At times, I have felt moral outrage at the way things have turned out—a sense that I had gotten "the shaft" for so long and "wasn't it about time things worked out for me?" With the merciful passage of time, however, I moved through the roughness of anger and into the softness of disappointment. With that came a feeling of humility. I saw that I was not the only one who suffered, that all humankind had, since the beginning of time, borne its unfair share of pain. I was no longer alone, then. I was part of something. Disappointment, for me, speaks directly to the "inner wound," my term for the feeling of being abandoned by God, or that existential pain of being separate from the things I most need or want.

Disappointment is a core feeling in childhood, since sooner or later our parents show up in ways that contradict what we expect. They disappoint us—at least half the time. As children, our days were generally divided between excitements and disappointments, and that division provided a big challenge for our parents, those two struggling adults probably lost in their own disappointments. How our parents modeled dealing with disappointment determined the tools we would have to deal with it as adults. From them, we may have learned that disappointment shouldn't be allowed, or that it meant a losing, a failure of some sort; or we learned that it was part and parcel of growing up—that something had to be left behind in order for something new to be discovered. Some fortunate few learned how to turn it into an opening or opportunity.

Certainly, disappointment is not usually the initial response to loss, especially the loss of a child. I wouldn't expect anyone to get to the heart of disappointment without going through fear, anger, confusion. If fact, if I were to have read or heard these descriptions during an angry, bitter, or resentful phase of my grieving, listening to them would have infuriated me. You can't be where you're not. On the other hand, I think that many of us also don't go far enough in our emotional journeying. It is possible to stay with one particular form of emotional expression just because it is familiar, or predictable, and not allow grief to roll on toward resignation, acceptance, and even beyond. Disappointment may be a bridge from the first phase of emotional pain to the second— the one that offers even greater possibilities.

I see disappointment as a basic ingredient in the soup we call human maturity. It is not a philosophical experience. "What is" is what happens, and it isn't fair, and it simply hurts. Yet, as with so many emotions, the honest acceptance of our woundedness and the disappointment that flows from it is, in our culture, greatly underestimated if not completely overlooked. For me, disappointment, since it lives at the roots of anger and sorrow, is the key to moving through life with grace.

My losses offer me profound lessons. I have the choice of using them to empower the bitterness and self-hate or to stoke the fire that will cauterize my wounds and ultimately heal me. I believe that is a choice that every human has.

One night, shortly after my second miscarriage, as I lay in bed feeling the grief of my loss, I began to experience the pain of every woman who has ever lost a relationship with a child, together with the pain of countless grieving men who were either standing by the women in sorrow or turned away in their own fear, confusion, and denial. Yet, despite its profound depth, this pain did not overwhelm me. Rather, I felt my loss as bittersweet, for this grief and sorrow were bonding me in a kindship with humankind.

I didn't resist the pain but simply allowed intense sadness to move through me, the way a strong wind moves through the branches of a tree. My heart began to ache in empathy with those who had known more heavy sorrows than my own, and I was filled with an abiding sense of compassion and love, sensing the universality of human suffering and the fellowship or sisterhood created by our woundedness.

In writing to a mother whose baby had died, the poet Redhawk captured the bittersweetness that Susan touched upon. His words remind us that it is possible to look upon even the most traumatic losses from a perspective that all things are beautiful.

FOR JANE, WHOSE BABY DIED

I am glad for her today
because she tasted something rare:
a Great Soul rested briefly in her womb,
received its warmth and comfort there.

A Great Soul enters where it chooses,
leaves freely when it pleases;
it does not give a damn for our desires.

It draws near for a moment,
bends low to hold us dearly,
breathes once upon the spark in us,
leaves a sheer trace of light
on the dark within the heart.

By this fragile flame
her way is lit;
on this gentle breath
she rises, slowly dresses,
goes about her morning work.
She does not breathe a word of it,
but feels the subtle beating in her heart
as she chops the vegetables,
stirs her coffee,
reaches softly for her lover in the night.

It is something rare
to labor long and well
so a Great Soul might draw near,
and I am glad for her today.

FAITH, HOPE, AND WHOLENESS

Faith and hope are both gifts and decisions. They come for the asking, from within ourselves or from some place of mystery beyond us; and they come as a result of a choice or self-declaration that we are ready for these attributes to characterize our lives. We decide who or what to put faith or hope in, and then we proceed to live out the consequences of those choices. If our realities don't match our expectations, we sometimes question the source of our faith or hope. Sometimes, especially during times of crisis, we may be so disappointed, if not enraged, with the outcome of events that we may be inclined to withdraw faith or hope, reinvest them somewhere else, or give up on them entirely. That's known as the crisis of faith, and it can be both frightening and liberating. But one way or another it is normal, and it is healthy—a way of reordering our fragmented parts and forcing us to choose our lives consciously, rather than being run by our early or random programming. But that happens slowly, over time. This part of the neutral zone can be agonizing unless you get some support.

Ideally, a crisis of faith will motivate us to seek out caring witnesses, other people who will listen as we explore and express our feelings, our doubts, our questions. We can also be asking ourselves to identify what the core beliefs are that underlie our questions and move our lives. (In the early stages, however, don't expect ease or clarity with questions of this nature. Writing is extremely helpful because it literally allows us to create the answers to our questions.) Once touched, these core beliefs have a power of their own. They generally serve to illuminate the path ahead, indicating where to place our next step.

Elisabeth Kubler-Ross, whose work I have mentioned, finds that the primary factor in determining the duration of our grief, and the health of our grief in general, is connection with a religious faith. In my experience, that doesn't have to mean only a belief in a particular church teaching, or even in a higher power, but can also include a practice that allows one to assign the loss within a broader, more universal context. That context-shift is decidedly possible for everyone. The power of a like-minded or like-spirited group to ease one over the difficult times cannot be underestimated. This is another benefit of associating with a religious faith. Strong family ties can do the same thing.

Most people cope with loss in the ways in which their parents did. If our mothers and dads were open and expressive in handling their own grief, if they informed us of the reality of life and death with a cosmology of hope, and if they held these painful mysteries as necessary mysteries, we have a greater chance of doing the same.

If they closed down around their pain, sought solace through addictive behavior, or adopted the euphemisms of their religious culture without question, we will be strongly influenced to do likewise—unless we make efforts do differently. That difference will be our willingness to stop, in our generation, the unconscious legacy of denial by doing our own grief work.

Laura's story, which follows, demonstrates how one woman drew strength and courage from her religious faith and the support of her family culture. It is the last story in this book, and the longest. But I have included the whole piece because Laura's is a classic story: it demonstrates all the stages of grief, including the crisis of faith and the resurrection that follows it.

Laura's story still brings me to tears, although I have read it dozens of times since Laura first told it to us. Reading it is valuable for that reason. My tears, your tears, help clear the path to the heart, thus connecting us to our own Source of faith and hope.

LAURA'S STORY

Celia was nine and nearing the end of third grade when she died. That was two years ago in June.

It all happened so fast. The first sign of anything questionable didn't show up until March, about three months before she died. Then two things happened. First, her disposition changed. She started getting feisty, argumentative.

The second sign was when she started to complain of not being able to focus on the blackboard at school. "Well, just ask the teacher if you can sit up closer," I suggested. You know how it is. Kids have complaints all the time.

Then it was her hearing. She didn't seem as if she were listening to me. "Oh, were you talking?" she would say quite innocently—when I would get her attention and look her in the face. But I kept thinking it was all just behavioral. Actually, as we learned later, all of her main senses were dulling rapidly. "When you go to school," I again offered naively, "ask the nurse to check your vision and hearing."

She complained of headaches and stomachaches more regularly then, too. It's shocking to note these things in retrospect. I remember one day she came home and told me that she fell down when she was walking home from school. "You tripped?" I inquired. "No, Mom," she said incredulously, "I just fell down." I thought it was so strange. Now I realize that she was gradually showing signs of losing it altogether. Celia was falling apart. That's when I finally took her for a neurological exam.

Our family doctor was a young fellow without much experience. He looked into her eyes and said, "I don't see anything." But a blood test showed signs of the Epstein-Barr virus, so we thought we had the answer at last. Actually, her symptoms could have fit into many different categories. We were so relieved to have found one.

We went home ready to start our plan of attack: "I'll just give her mega-vitamins and build up her immune system," I resolved. "That will beat this thing!"

But it didn't. She started getting weaker, and sicker, and throwing up her food. Things got so severe that she had no energy. She would sleep and wake up exhausted. She could play for only a short time and then have to lie down. This went on for almost three weeks. As hard as we were working to help her, nothing was pepping her up. It was the end of the school year, and I remember feeling afraid that she wouldn't be able to finish her school work enough to graduate from third grade.

She was discouraged, too, and would sometimes cry. "Mom, what's happening to me?" she would ask. "We just need to get rid of this bug in your system," I would reply. I couldn't imagine that it wasn't just a long, drawn-out virus or something.

I would ask her about her strange behavior, too. "Celia, why are you acting this way?"

"I don't know, Mom," she would say with a look of confusion. "I just can't help it." It was as if she were just out of control.

At the end of May I took the children down to my sister's house. She had a pool, and as soon as the children got there they immediately started playing in the water, even Celia. But after only about ten minutes she came into the house and went into the bedroom to lie down. "Oh, I feel so sick," she said. She was exhausted.

My sister took one look at her, looked me straight

in the eye and said, "Laura, there is something really wrong here." That was the shock I needed. I had to admit that she wasn't getting better. I had to get her in for another examination.

The second doctor was older and had more experience. At this point her right eye was moving inward, and she could hardly do the tests. When he looked into her eyes, he saw it. Water, bulging behind her eyes. Actually, it was a massive buildup of spinal fluid. But the doctor didn't give me many of the details. Instead, he just took me aside and said that we needed to get down to Children's Hospital as soon as possible and have Magnetic Resonance Imaging (MRI) done. This procedure is a state-of-the-art brain scan.

He was serious. I was frightened. He made it clear that we shouldn't wait. "What are we talking about here?" I asked him. "Could it really be that serious?" He was noncommittal. "Something neurological going on in the brain. . . ." is all I remember him saying. I got the message. I went home and prepared the family, making arrangements to have my other three children taken care of. I called my husband, who was out of town working, and he came right home. Then I packed enough clothes for a few days, picked up Celia's best friend (who wanted to go with us), and left for the hospital.

The next day, a Tuesday, Celia was admitted to Children's Hospital.

I was deeply scared and apprehensive, and as we were settling her in her room, I was dying inside. But I never let on. When my fears got too heavy, I just went into the bathroom and shed some tears.

Things started moving fast, then. The technicians did some initial blood work on her, then moved her up to another floor for more intensive tests. Within a matter of hours she was taken in for the MRI. During all this time I waited in her room.

It was such a strange time. My older sister was getting married that week, and I remembered thinking that when things had settled down here I could leave Celia for a few hours and go to visit my sister. Maybe even get to the wedding. Funny how we make our plans sometimes.

Forty-five minutes later they brought Celia back to the room. When I saw the doctor's face, something broke inside me. He had a very serious look. "Let's go find a room where we can talk," he said. I knew it had to be bad, but in addition I was so shocked that I couldn't think what he was going to say.

"Your little girl is very seriously ill," he said. "She has a tumor on the brain stem, and it is very large. In fact, I've never seen one so large." I sat there trying to absorb his words, trying to keep control, but shaking.

"Are we talking about cancer?" I finally blurted out when I could form some words. "Cancer of the brain?"

"Yes," he said as he nodded his head. Then he took a chalkboard and drew me an illustration of what was going on, showing me how the tumor had grown within the spinal cord and how it was backing up the cerebral spinal fluid.

"How serious is this?" I asked again, still grasping at straws.

He explained to me that Celia's tumor was the most fatal type of brain tumor. It literally cuts off the senses, one by one—all of them.

"From what I've seen," he went on, "children with this type of tumor live about two months to one year." He was offering me no escape from having to confront the news.

"You mean to tell me that anyone who has this

tumor is not alive today?" I couldn't believe what I was hearing.

"That's right," he said.

I sat there for a moment in silence and then said, "Can I cry?"

"I certainly would," said the doctor. So I lifted my hands to my face and allowed myself to weep.

"What are our options?" I asked him when I could form the words.

"To make Celia more comfortable by helping to relieve that pressure caused by the spinal fluid," he went on. "We'll put in a shunt to carry off the fluid, and then test the tumor for malignancy." I recall very clearly that he said there was only a five percent chance that something could go wrong in the biopsy. But that was it. "The best thing we can do is to give her a quality of life for the time remaining—a few weeks to a few months," he reiterated.

News like that just bowls you over. You can't believe it. That relief was all we could hope for? That cure wasn't even a part of the picture? You can't believe that what you are hearing is real.

The doctor told me that this was the kindest type of cancer. Because it gradually cut off her senses, it was as if she were given anesthesia. Except for the headaches caused by the fluid build-up, she had no pain, and throughout it all she never appeared frightened, even when she went down for the surgery. She exuded a confidence that helped the rest of us through it.

Mercifully, there was so much to do that it gave me a sense of purpose. I started making calls to family and friends, telling people to come down, and within hours long distance calls came in from all over. We have quite a network of family.

When I finally got through to my husband, I told

him straight and simple. "It is a brain tumor, and it is
fatal." I could hear him over the phone. He just
broke into sobs.

Laura paused to rest for a few moments, drink some
water, and ask Susan and me if her story was what we wanted for the book. After my assurance, she continued:

"I am Mormon. And we have a strong belief in
priesthood blessings. So as soon as I got the news I
had a brother-in-law and another man come in and do
the blessings for her.
    The rest of the family soon started arriving, and
the phone was ringing off the wall. Meanwhile, Celia
wanted to know what was going on. "Did they find out
what is wrong with me?" she asked. And I explained
that the doctor was going to give her an operation to
help her headaches. She accepted that without further questioning. I always tried to make it very simple so that she wouldn't get upset.
    The next day, Wednesday, the surgery was sched-
uled, and many family members joined us in Celia's
room that morning. My sister asked me if we could
get the video camera and take some pictures of Celia.
And of course I agreed. I am so glad we did. None of
us knew that this would be her last conversation with
us. And this video has turned out to be the most precious possession I have. All in all, Celia was in good
spirits, even joking with us, and we had a strong
familial experience of unity.
    Then, in the presurgery room, trying to be happy
and positive, I kissed her goodbye and said "We'll see
you in a couple of hours."
    The surgeon told us that the operation would last
for only an hour and a half, so after two hours we
began to get nervous.

Nearly three hours after she went in, we learned
that the surgeon wanted to talk to us.

"There was a complication," he said. *Complication*—the word was incomprehensible after what we'd
been through. This was supposed to be a routine procedure! It seems that as the surgeons were going in
for the biopsy, a piece of the tissue being removed
adhered to a major vessel. As they pulled it away she
"started hemorrhaging badly". . ."lost a lot of blood". . .
"only thing we could do to save her life". . . "open her
skull". . ."cauterize the vein". . ."the bleeding stopped
miraculously". . ."don't know why."

"Only clue I had," the doctor spoke with great compassion, "is that the bleeding stopped because she was
not ready to go." We had almost lost her.

As I walked into the intensive care unit, seeing her
as she was, I just about fainted. She looked exactly as
if someone had been carving on her skull. It was more
than I could take. I started to feel extremely sick to
my stomach, and I just walked out. I couldn't believe
what they had done to my little girl.

She was on a respirator, with a tube going down
her throat, and still on anesthesia. As she slowly
aroused, she squeezed my hand three times. I almost
lost control then: she had used our little secret hand-
shake—three squeezes: *I, love, you.*

The following Monday she was dead—less than a
full week after we had entered the hospital. We came
there for tests, but she never left.

Every day of that timeless week was different. In
fact, every hour was different. Sometimes she was
alert, looking at me with questions in her eyes about
what was happening to her. Then she would lapse into
coma. She gradually got weaker, developed fevers and
pneumonia, and finally, her strength just left.

Laura paused again to catch her breath. She had been
speaking for nearly two hours, and she still had more to say.

When you're in an acute trauma like that, even
with all the faith I thought I had, it is still confusing.
"How could this happen? How could you do this to
us?" I lamented to God. "Don't we already have our
hands full?" I was feeling tremendously burdened.
Our second child, another little girl, is mentally
retarded. With her it is constant—the illnesses, the
doctors, the adjustments. Dealing with her is such a
massive challenge, and I'm faced with grieving something every day. As a family, we can't do the things
that other people can do. We can't go on trips, we can
hardly take her out in public much. I constantly have
to face and find answers to so many questions. But,
that's another story—enough for a whole book in
itself.

I have to say that the only way I coped with Celia's
death was through my knowledge of and faith in the
purpose of life and in what goes on after life. We
believe in the resurrection, so we knew that losing
Celia was not the end of all ends. Still, it is difficult to
really grasp that we are not going to get her back
here. This is permanent, for now. Not just for two
weeks, as if she'd gone away for camp or something.
Not just as if she'd left for college. Permanent. There
were times when I hurt so much, I didn't think I could
bear it. But then something happened to change that.

I pray. We are a very praying family. And during
one of those incredibly hard times I prayed, "Lord
you're going to have to give me something to get
through." And he did.

My sister-in-law told me an amazing incident—
reluctantly, since she wasn't sure how I would take it,

or whether I would believe it. As she experienced it, during the time that Celia was in coma, the child's spirit, with the assistance of my grandmother (who is dead), visited my sister-in-law, who at the time was out in her back yard gardening. It was only a two-minute visit, but Celia's spirit communicated a huge amount of information—information that gave me tremendous strength and consoled me. I took this incident as a special religious experience. Before it happened, I was in such pain that I didn't want to see anything to remind me of Celia. I wanted to clean out her things and put them all away. But, after hearing this, my grieving changed radically. It was the difference between night and day.

There was a funny thing about Celia: ever since she was little she had an intuitive connection to the spirit world. She would write stories about angels, or about relatives who had passed away, and her teachers were always pleased with these clever stories. So this "visitation" seemed a natural thing for her to do.

The funeral was actually uplifting. Many of Celia's friends were there, too, and these children would come up to the casket, look at her and just bawl. I was able to console them by saying, "It's okay." And I meant it.

If the sadness of a funeral and a death can be mixed with happiness, it was that kind of an experience. Because of the strength I had received I was able to get involved in preparing her burial. I helped dress her. I fixed her hair. All those little things finalized her life on earth. It was necessary, and I was so glad to be able to finish my responsibility.

During the funeral I was not very emotional. So many people were there that their presence took my mind off myself. It wasn't until a few weeks after-

ward that the grieving settled in. Before that I was so
supported, so cared for—but suddenly all the relatives went home, and life was there waiting. Then the
real void came in.

That first year after the loss was like one long
anniversary. Suddenly, it's her next birthday, or the
start of school, and you see her friends going off on
the bus, and you remember that she is not going to do
that. Or it's Halloween. The first of anything, really,
is especially hard. But after the first year, it was not
half as difficult.

We keep very open about Celia's death with our
other children, and they seem to be doing quite well.
Sometimes I hear their concern or fear about it,
though. My third child asked me recently if she would
get sick, as Celia did.

The only guilt I have is for getting after her for
behaving so ridiculously, and the way I disciplined
her. I feel badly about that. She was really dying,
and I was getting after her. Why did I do that?

I've been able to shed tears, to feel lonely or sad.
Unfortunately, my husband still has a much harder
time dealing with Celia's death than I do. He doesn't
share his feelings as well.

I really am at peace, though. I feel that she is in a
place where she is busy. She is progressing. And
occasionally I have felt her essence around me—some
mental connection.

I asked Laura to talk about her own childhood, curious
to find clues that suggested the reason behind her healthy
grief. She knew the answer to that one without even thinking about it.

I was the youngest of eight children, and my father
died while I was a child. When I recall my feelings

around that time, I realize that my mother gave us a very healthy concept of death. It wasn't a taboo subject. My father was in the hospital for quite a while before he died, and I'd ask mother, "Has Heavenly Father taken Daddy yet?" And she would sit down and talk to me about it. My childhood was so rare, so emotionally stable, that I feel almost guilty when I see what terrible traumas other people have gone through. It makes me want to just reach out to them. I want to pass that healthy attitude about life and death on to my children in this generation.

My mother was very supportive when Celia died. She allowed me to grieve as much as I needed to. She, too, holds the big picture that our religious faith has given us: when you know the whole process, it is much easier to cope.

So many people can't face the reality of grief and separation. I think they make themselves suffer so much more than is necessary. Death is hard, but it can be less painful if you know that it's part of a plan.

I really believe that there is a time to leave this earthly life, that the Deity knows my family and knows the circumstances and the reason my child was taken. Right now, I am living on faith. After this life, I will live in pure knowledge. I know that, as long as we keep God's laws, we will be together as a family.

There are worse things than death.

Even if you feel that you have no formal faith, you can hold fast to any recollection of innocence or love, within yourself or in another, as a source of inspiration and courage during times of grief. Such threads of remembrance hold the potential of leading one to the doorway of a broader context—the experience of seeing and accepting grief as integral to life. In the thirteenth century, the poet Rumi, an ecstatic mystic, sang of the awesome Love he had glimpsed: a love that excludes none, regardless of faithlessness. In this poem he invites us all to simply turn in the direction of Love's door.

> *Come again, please, come again,*
> *Whoever you are.*
> *Religious, infidel, heretic or pagan.*
> *Even if you promised a hundred times,*
> *And a hundred times you broke your promise,*
> *This door is not the door*
> *Of hopelessness and frustration.*
> *This door is open for everybody.*
> *Come, come as you are.*[1]

FOR JOURNALLING

These selected writing topics will encourage you to apply to your own life the subjects covered in this chapter.

1. In finding the word "disappointment" to characterize her grief, Susan was able to make many more distinctions about the pain she felt, and its purpose. What is the word (or words) that characterize your grief? You may wish to try on several before you settle on one or two. You may, for example, choose *emptiness, abandonment, breathlessness, longing.*

    Once you have found a word that "speaks" to your grief, write about it and all its implications for you. Don't neglect to consider what this "word" is teaching you. Perhaps you will want to draw or paint your feelings in relationship to that word.

---

[1] Mevlana Celaleddin Rumi, translation by Nevit O. Ergin, *Crazy As We Are* (Prescott, AZ: Hohm Press, 1992). Used with permission.

2. Bill Bridges writes about the "neutral zone" as a time for stalling, for doing nothing, for going away, for trying to see the big picture, for learning about surrender, for waiting, for dreams, for the unconscious, for asking the questions "What next?" What are some of the characteristics of your neutral zone? Are these things you have blamed yourself for? Can you write about them as if they were necessary steps in your grief? Do that.

3. The crisis of loss can challenge our once-firm foundations, leaving us with the sense that we no longer believe in anything. One way to remember the things we hold true about life is to write a credo. The word *credo* is Latin and means "I believe." A credo may be an extensive philosophical treatise or a series of phrases much like a poem or song.

Writing a list of some of your beliefs may help you identify some of your core beliefs—the ones that underlie the rest, like the belief that human life is valuable, if not sacred.

To begin your credo, consider what you believe about the following topics: life (human, animal, plant . . .), the earth and our responsibility for it, God or religion, suffering, children. As you list your beliefs, realize that your credo is not static. It changes as you do, sometimes day by day. So don't be afraid to write your credo for today, knowing that you can change it tomorrow.

If one or more of your beliefs surprise you or provoke you to want to explore further, discontinue the listing and start writing about that belief. Take your time in doing this exercise. Take as long as you care to. You could begin, for example:

"About life, I believe. . . ."

As always, whenever you do any journal writing, finish your work by responding to the following statement:

"As a result of doing this writing I. . . ."

The final phase of the grief process involves reinvesting the interest, attention, and energy that was directed toward the loss into new, life-affirming relationships or activities. Before that, however, we need to tie up some loose ends.

10

Ways and Means

A WOMAN TAKES herself to the mountains and spends a day alone, reading the journals of her life, remembering the child she lost at birth.

In the middle of the afternoon she carefully digs a hole at the base of an impressive pine. She burns a paper on which she has written tender words of good-bye, then places the charred scraps in the hole, along with a few collected items—a seashell, a pink ribbon, a photograph—and a few more treasures that she has found during her walk— a flower, a stone, a piece of bone. Each one means something to her. In burying them, she makes them sacred.

With her bare hands she pushes the dirt over these symbols of her loss and softly sings a song. It is a personal song, one she used to sing during her pregnancy. A song that soothed her baby in the womb.

She sits for a long time and contemplates this tiny

grave. It hurts to remember, but it hurts much more to forget. She cries and feels cleansed.

As the sun drops out of sight, she rises and walks slowly back to her car, her ritual complete.

She has done this before, in a variety of ways, and she will do it again, perhaps years from now. She will grieve; she will honor the wound that opened her heart; she will move on.

*   *   *

The hundreds and thousands of us who grieve the loss of children or potential children will do that grief work each in our own way, according to our own timing. Yet today, with a deepened appreciation of the process of healing through grieving, we have available to us numerous resources that honor the needs of body, mind, emotions, and soul. While they don't diminish the pain, these resources can help us deal with it in ways that promote healthy integration and allow us to move forward in our lives instead of remaining stuck in a seemingly endless cycle of depression, or fear, or anger, or guilt. Far from crushing us, or leaving us crazy, our pain can be grappled with and finally understood in a way that bears the potential of opening us to a deeper level of meaning in life.

Using a ritual, like the simple, personal process described above, is one potent form of grieving that is receiving widespread attention and use. Journal-writing is another, one that we have encouraged throughout this book because of its proven effectiveness. Serious journalling can actually improve health. A study conducted at Southern Methodist University, for example, found that those who wrote about their serious illnesses, expressing both facts and emotions, showed more improved immune system functioning, determined through blood testing, than those who merely wrote on trivial subjects. This chapter will remind you of what you may already know but have forgotten and will encourage you to make use of a variety of readily-available resources that may prove not only helpful but invaluable as you begin, or more likely continue, your grief work.

I wish you courage, strength, and genuine joy in that work.

HELPING THE BODY IN GRIEF

Grieving tends to deplete your physical resources as it does your emotional energy, and for that reason it is important to give your body additional attention during such stressful times.

Stress doesn't automatically lead to illness, since some people actually thrive on stress. But when the stress is accompanied by depression, sadness, anger, confusion, or other draining emotional states, it tends to weaken the immune system functioning, making the grieving person more susceptible to disease.

The more you can get the body moving, and the more you can nurture what health you have, in life-enhancing ways, the greater your resistance will be.

Care for your body by:
- avoiding addictive substances as much as possible. It is a common tendency to increase our dependence on coffee, tobacco, or alcohol when we are under stress. Yet these substances will actually increase the stress the body is already bearing, so use them cautiously.
- getting adequate sleep, or even more sleep than usual. Don't feel guilty about using sleep as an adjunct to your healing. It is very therapeutic.

- eating a balanced meal whenever you can. Since your whole system is often in turmoil as you do deeper grief work, and you may find that you are using food for its "mother-love" value (something that is understandable), attempt to balance that reaction by eating at least one healthy meal a day. Eat fresh fruits, fresh vegetables, and whole grains whenever possible. Try to avoid foods that will require extra work to digest, like heavy fats, which are a challenge to the liver; or too much bread, pasta, or other refined carbohydrates, which tend to clog up the intestines and will fill you up without supplying much nutritional assistance.

- drinking lots of good water. Flushing out your system with water will help keep your emotional "body" from stagnating as much it will add to your physical well-being. Adding a little fruit juice to your water (three ounces of juice per quart of water) may make it more pleasant to take in large quantities. If possible, drink eight big glasses a day. Or get in the habit of carrying a water bottle around and drinking regularly throughout the day.

- putting more conscious attention into your breathing, to supply you with the oxygen you need to keep your head clear and your metabolism balanced.

  Since your body tends to carry grief in the chest, throat, and lung region, these areas may constrict when your organism is threatened. You may actually be restricting your breathing even more in an unconscious, but vain, attempt to keep yourself from feeling any more pain. If you feel short of breath or as if you've "just had the wind knocked out of you," be assured that this, too, is common.

  Take a full breath now, not by gasping for it but simply by exhaling as fully as you can, actually forc-

ing the last bits of air out of your lungs. Then let
nature take its course. Air will rush in to fill up the
vacuum you have created. A fuller inhalation will
be the result. Do this two or three times, whenever
you think of it. Or put up a few signs around your
house that say: *Breathe.* Whenever you notice one
of the signs, pause and do the exercise suggested.

Allow yourself to sigh, as audibly and deeply as
you wish, whenever the thought or the pain arises.
Sighing is normal and will help you to breathe.

Open the windows, or step outside, several times
a day, to refresh yourself with breathing.

- exercising regularly, and as vigorously as appropriate for you. This is one of the greatest helps in
breathing better, and it also assists you in burning
up excess anxiety and in invigorating a sluggish
system. Walk vigorously, even if only around your
house or apartment. Or put on some music and
dance by yourself. Use a mini-trampoline, if you
have one, to add variety to your exercise. Outdoor
exercise—walking, jogging, bike-riding, tennis, or
swimming—will be extremely beneficial.

In my grief classes I encourage dancing as a form
of exercise. I use carefully selected rock music, and
other music with a primal beat, to help students
move out of the mind and into the body, particularly
the abdomen, legs, and feet. This kind of dancing is
not necessarily pretty or smooth. It can be grinding,
pounding, and quite cathartic. That's precisely why I
use it. Particular types of music (my favorite rock
group is an Arizona band called "liars, gods, and beggars"—see the Resource Guide) force us to make
contact with the ground under our feet and to open
energy pathways in parts of the body that may be
blocked with unexpressed emotion. I encourage my

students to "dance" their emotions—fear, confusion, anger, sadness, whatever.

If you decide to use music for this purpose, I suggest that, to get maximum benefit, you use it several times a week. Using the same music each day will create a familiarity and a sense of safety that will encourage you to "go deeper" or express more each time.

Use gardening, raking leaves, or simply washing windows in place of regular exercise, but do *something*, if possible, several times a week, stretching/relaxing. Combined with active movement, stretching, which increases flexibility and aids in overall relaxation, is a boon to your system, as it works through grief. Yoga is one method that is particularly useful, since it combines bodily stretches with regulated breathing exercises. If nothing else, pause frequently in the course of your day and stretch yourself, to relieve the tightness that the body will accumulate from emotional stress.

For help in relaxing, use music that nurtures you, even if it makes you cry. The added release of your tears will relieve some of your stress.

Relax in the bathtub, or under a shower. Water is one of the most healing substances at our immediate disposal.

- letting yourself be touched. Ask your trusted friends to hug you or simply hold you as necessary and appropriate. If possible, treat yourself to a full-body, therapeutic massage on a regular basis, or at least as a special treat once in a while. Ask friends for referrals, or check the bulletin boards at your local health-food store for the names of licensed massage therapists in your area.
- contacting the earth, the water, the sky. The natural cycles of nature are cycles of birth, growth, decay,

death, regeneration. They instruct us in the organic
processes of life and death, and they can help us put
our grief into a larger perspective. Give yourself
the gift of nature as you grieve by taking yourself
out under the sky. Walk along a beach. Hike a
mountain trail. Sit within a grove of trees or in the
midst of a garden. Lie down in a meadow, on a green
lawn, or across a large rock. Let the sunlight touch
your skin. Stand in moonlight. Gaze at the stars.
Speak your grief to the heavens, the waters, the
soil, the trees. Listen to their response.

EMOTIONAL HELP AS YOU GRIEVE

Feelings will take on a life of their own, usually with sorry
consequences, if they are not dealt with or expressed. The
blocked energy of sadness, rage, or fear will not simply "go
away." It will lodge itself in the muscles, the joints, the
organs, as pain and disease. It will send distress signals to
the brain, which will alter the body's ability to fight infection.
It will cause stomach ulcers, skin eruptions, headaches,
digestive complications, and much more.

As if the physical implications were not enough, emotional stress will take the color out of life, draining our world of
meaning and purpose. It will influence our decision-making,
our communications, and our child-raising practices. Some
people will withdraw from relationships, while others will pile
one relationship upon another, all in an attempt to relieve the
pain of emotional anguish caused by a child-related loss.

Utilizing emotional "steam-valves" to periodically help
in relieving the pressure that builds up with grief is the best
preventive treatment. Here are some of the most powerful
tools I know of:

- Use support groups—that is, self-help groups. This
  movement of "people helping people" has in recent
  years swept the United States. It is now possible
  to find, in every major city and even in many small
  towns, groups of people meeting regularly to talk
  about their common loss or illness. While support
  groups should not be considered a substitute for
  those who need professional psychological or psy-
  chiatric therapy, they are an appropriate adjunct to
  individual counseling.

  There are many existing groups for: parents
  who experience a miscarriage, stillbirth, or early
  infant death (SIDS); men and women dealing with
  infertility (RESOLVE); women and men making
  decisions about abortion (Planned Parenthood and
  Right to Life); women who have had abortions
  (Planned Parenthood and others); women in crisis
  of any kind (Women's Resource Centers);
  Compassionate Friends, a national organization for
  parents who have lost a child through death;
  fathers who have trouble in securing custody
  rights; people who were abused as children—sexually, physically, or emotionally; parents of run-
  aways; and more.

  Check your local hospital, your church, or the
  Social Service section of your phone book to find
  out the types of support groups that exist in your
  community. In some cities the newspaper will occasionally list all the support groups and the dates
  and time of regular meetings, or will include these
  in their "Meetings" or "Events" sections.

  Without a structured group it is still possible to
  benefit from sharing your story with a group of
  friends, preferably of your own sex, as long as the
  members are willing to listen without judging you

for your strong emotions or opinions or trying to "make you better" by giving you unasked-for advice or consolation. The idea is to allow yourself to explore your path through pain, speaking your own advice and consolation as appropriate or not. This book, and others listed in its bibliography, will be helpful in guiding you through this process. Read a chapter together, and then spend your time talking about your responses to what you've read. My own experience in telling my story to caring witnesses, and in being a witness to hundreds of others, has convinced us that this approach to healing is one of the most valuable, if not essential.

- Use professional help: therapists, counselors, pastoral counselors, psychologists, psychiatrists—all of these titles describe the services of professionals who may help you throughout your grieving, or at particularly difficult junctures along the way. Therapy is not reserved for seriously disturbed people, and in some cases the stigma formally attached to "seeing a shrink" has given way to therapy being a status symbol ("as my shrink says. . ."). It is my experience that, at some points in life, almost everyone can benefit from the services of a professionally-trained therapist.

  While the phone book will provide a listing of professionals, under "Psychologists" or "Counselors," it is preferable to get a referral from someone you know and trust who has experience with the therapist you are considering. Ask friends or church members.

  Today, many therapists have special training in dealing with issues of grief and loss, and the best way to find out about their training and experience is to arrange an interview in lieu of a first session.

Be an informed consumer and ask questions of your
therapist to determine how much background he or
she has in dealing with issues like yours.

DETERMINING IF YOU NEED PROFESSIONAL HELP

If you are questioning whether you need help or not, I recommend that you seek it. It is always better to be safe than sorry.
Often, one or two sessions with a trained psychotherapist or
pastoral counselor (check with your church for referrals) is all
you will need to help you re-establish a firm footing.

Definitely seek professional help if:
- you are having regular thoughts about suicide or
  about the desirability of illness or death for yourself.
- your emotional reactions are regularly or consistently violent, rageful, aggressive, or abusive
  towards others or yourself.
- you have a history of alcoholism, drug or other substance abuse, or an eating disorder.
- you feel no energy and little joy, or have been depressed for a period longer than a year after your loss.
- you are constantly preoccupied with thoughts or
  feelings of guilt, unworthiness, or shame, or continue to blame yourself for your loss, even after two or
  three years.
- your marriage or other primary relationship is in
  jeopardy.
- other people have suggested that you seek professional help.

Professional help can be beneficial if:
- you find it difficult to talk to family or friends about
  your loss.

- you feel lonely or depressed.
- you are afraid that your feelings and behavior are abnormal.
- you have no support system, or you wish to learn how to build one.
- you are having a hard time managing your life financially, keeping your attention on your job, handling the responsibilities of your home and other family members.
- you are confused about what decision would be "right" for you.
- you are having regular conflicts with your spouse, partner, other children, or family members.
- your loss has reminded you of a trauma in your childhood or earlier life, and you want to use this opportunity to further your overall healing or your personal growth.

DEALING WITH STRONG OR STRANGE EMOTIONS

One of the most disturbing aspects of grief is that you often feel as if you are "going crazy" and don't know what to do about all the powerful emotions and confusing energies, or lack of energy, in your body. Be assured, first of all, that strong or strange emotions and confused states are the norm in the early stages of your grief (the first year) and will visit you periodically throughout your life, especially in the few years after your loss.

Yet strong emotion can be used to help you heal. If it is allowed, rather than repressed or denied, the energy of anger, fear, sadness, confusion, and relief will move through you like waves washing the seashore. It will ebb and flow. It will sometimes take you back into very early stages of your life, offering you the opportunity to mourn the losses you didn't mourn at the time. That has been the whole premise of this book.

While there are literally hundreds of helpful ways of dealing, on your own, with strong emotion, we suggest a few that we have found to be most effective.

Move strong emotions by:
- exercising, dancing, moving or working vigorously. (See suggestions in previous section.)
- screaming—into a pillow; in an empty house; in your parked car with the windows rolled up; and in similar isolated situations.
- crying. The ability and willingness to express tears, even though you fear that once they start they will never stop, is one of your greatest assets in the grief process. If tears arise, let them flow. They will stop of their own accord. Let them cleanse and heal you.
- nourishing or consoling your "inner child." The part of you that becomes frightened by strong and strange emotions may need some consolation throughout grieving. As you do this grief work you will simultaneously need to acknowledge and honor this fearful, hurting inner child. Many people today are making use of soft, overstuffed toy animals, hugging them for security in times of threatening flashbacks, taking them to bed, or carrying them around in the car. The "teddy bear" or other animal becomes a much needed security and helps the over-adapted adult part of the personality to relax a bit so that the child can come out to play.

  Other ways to nourish this child are through particular types of play; a ride on a swing, a trip down a slide, a day at the beach, a hike in the woods, or a

day spent going fishing. There is also dancing, art-
work, hot bubble baths, and snuggling up with a
good book before a roaring fire. The idea here is to
let your imagination direct you in activities that are
enjoyable and help you to feel secure and loved—
especially by yourself,

See the Bibliography for books that may help
you deepen your relationship with the inner child.

* drawing, painting, sculpting (or simply pounding)
  with clay. Since many of us find difficulty in
  expressing our emotions in words, it is extremely
  helpful to use non-verbal means, especially art, to
  access and express this powerful and important
  energy. My students constantly report their surprise with the effectiveness of drawing or painting
  a picture of their loss, their fears, their sadness,
  their hopes. I suggest that they start by making
  the biggest mess they can on their paper, and that
  they do this for at least two pictures. That helps
  break any old messages about the way "art is supposed to be beautiful." Following that, I encourage
  them to choose colors that represent whatever
  emotional state they are experiencing and to simply let those colors move across the paper, doing
  whatever they want to do.

  These helpful beginnings are often enough to
  bring about temporary pain relief, increased clarity,
  and even a broader perspective or sense of inner
  peace due to the release of built-up stress. (For
  specific exercises, see the works of Lucia
  Capacchione listed in the Bibliography.)

* journalling and writing. As I have mentioned
  throughout this book, writing allows you to access
  your inner wisdom, something that may seem very
  far away when you are in the midst of the pain of

your loss. Review Chapter 2 if you want additional motivation for writing. I also recommend that you go back through the chapters regularly and work with the exercises provided. Two of my favorite approaches to writing are: responding to incomplete sentences and letter-writing. Take a few minutes now to complete these incomplete sentences in as many ways as you care to:

1. As I look back over the past few months I . . .

2. I have felt much worse when:

3. I have felt somewhat better when:

4. I wish:

5. I want:

6. I will:

7. As a result of doing this exercise, I am aware:

Letter writing includes addressing yourself to a real friend or imaginary support person, telling your story, expressing your needs, talking about your questions.

Letter writing is also one of the most effective ways of handling the unfinished business connected with a child-related loss. Perhaps you feel specific pain at the thought that your lost child never got to know you. A letter that explains who you are, what you value, what you wanted for your child, and so on, will help you clarify feelings that might otherwise simply swim around uncollected in your consciousness. Letters of this nature can then be symbolically burned, buried, or saved for reading on special occasions, as a way of creating some closure. (See the section below on Ritual.)

- writing with the non-dominant hand. This technique has been adopted by many therapists and systems that encourage getting in touch with the repressed parts of yourself as a mode of healing old wounds and supporting yourself in dealing with current ones. Writing with "the other hand" frequently reveals surprising information and almost always provokes feelings that need expression.

  Try this: Take a large sheet of paper, and at the top, using your dominant hand and whatever writing implement you wish, write the heading: "These are some of the things that are just *hard to bear* right now in my life." Then, using your "other hand" and whatever writing implement you prefer, make a list of the things that are hard for you. Consider these responses to be coming from a part of yourself that needs to be heard.

  To take this exercise the next step, have a dialogue between your two "hands" by letting the dominant hand question the "child" about what was written, and then allowing the child to answer the questions. For more on this exciting and revealing process see *Recovery of Your Inner Child* by Lucia Capacchione (New York: Fireside, Simon and Schuster), 1991.

SPIRITUAL RESOURCES

- Prayer. For me, prayer is very ordinary. It is basically an experience of remembering my connection to God and God's connection to me. Whether you relate to the word "God" or not, you may profit, especially during times of grief, by taking a little time out of your busy work schedule to simply think about, rest in, or remember your connection to something in the Universe that is larger than you are. Going to God with our pain, or (as the Twelve Step Programs word it), admitting "we were powerless . . . and that our lives had become unmanageable . . . (we) came to believe that a Power greater than ourselves could restore us to sanity. . .(we) made a decision to turn our will and our lives over to the care of God as we understood Him." Making these declarations is an effective way of relieving the burden of believing that we have to carry our pain completely alone.

  Intense grief will commonly cause one to question any relationship with God, since people often blame God for their loss. So if this is true for you, do not be alarmed. This kind of extreme turmoil can be spiritually transformational, since it calls upon

us to die to all our old concepts of "God" so that the
raw reality of God, or the Ultimate Higher Power,
can be born within us.

- Ritual. As a culture in the United States we have
very little meaningful ritual and are in fact more
likely to consider ritual as something empty or
devoid of heart. The unpleasant memory of early
exposure to religious ritual in church has, in many
cases, soured this form of expression for us.

  Yet, from many corners, perhaps sparked by the
interest in Native American folkways, a resurgence
of ritual is emerging. In simple, personal ways,
more people are symbolically marking the significant events of their lives, their joys as well as their
sorrows, with some activity or gesture. There are
an infinite variety of ways to tangibly acknowledge
and then seal the connections among body, emotions, earth forces, Divine elements and powers,
thoughts, dreams, and hopes. That is precisely
what ritual does.

  Ritual takes the ordinary stuff of everyday life—
the earth, a letter, a flower, a candle, a bowl of
water, a meal, a walk in the woods—and, by applying simple attention to it, raises that object or
event to the symbolic level. Here it becomes a key
in a previously locked door, a map to a formerly
uncharted territory. With attention we simply
remember the essential sacredness of all things in
creation. With ritual we invoke this sacredness as a
means of healing ourselves, others, and our world.

- Practice forgiveness. At some point you will come
to realize that you are holding something against
yourself or others. You will face your own brokenness and begin to see a similar brokenness in others, and that will be a moment of spiritual awaken-

ing. Usually, however, these moments don't last.
That is why I speak of forgiveness as a practice.

Forgiveness is not something that we necessarily accomplish as much as it is something we intend
and then practice. We may not *feel* forgiving, but
that is not necessarily the point. Forgiveness is a
decision, not a feeling. In some cases it is a decision
to move out of hell, because blame, victimization,
hatred of self or others, is terribly painful. Once
that decision is made, we must renew it frequently
and wait patiently. We live into forgiveness, over
years; our intention actually draws forgiveness to
us.

- Dreams. As I was writing the final chapters of this
  book I had a most wonderful dream. In it I gave
  birth to a child, a boy baby named Andrew (a name
  of Greek origin, which means "strong"). I not only
  experienced sensations of giving birth, I also experienced holding and nursing the child. Then I
  watched him grow and finally mature into a strong,
  attractive young man. When I awoke I knew that I
  had a child in some domain of existence; some
  would call it the "spirit world." I just knew I had a
  spiritual child, and that, like a guardian angel, he
  was available to love and support me. Of course,
  Andrew is myself. But the dream took on a life of
  its own and allowed me to joyfully celebrate the
  new life that is being born in my every moment.

  Dreams may be a source of tremendous consolation as you grieve, even if they are also painful.
  You may dream of the lost child. In your dream you
  may feel a great sense of relief, believing that your
  dream is real and that now you have your child
  back again. That will certainly provide a bittersweet moment when you awake. These moments

help us to grieve. Sometimes they even give us much needed information, "messages" from or about our loved ones.

An experienced therapist can assist you in using your dreams for personal growth and to further your healing. There are also many fine books available on the subject, if you care to do this processing on your own. For suggestion, see the Bibliography.

Service. Reaching out to others, not to forget your pain but because you know how hard it is, is one of the most effective ways to put your own grief in perspective.

IN CONCLUSION

"She used to say that everybody has to become a mother—in fact, everything must become mother," the young man said. He was speaking of the woman who had recently died, Dina Rees, a medical doctor, spiritual teacher, renowned healer, and mother of ten children, who had lived near Freiburg, Germany.

I was in Freiburg doing research on remarkable women: saints, mystics, healers, both living and dead. Having met Dina in 1988, I was left with an indelible memory of one of the most powerful and yet loving women I had ever encountered. Now, anxious to speak with some of her closest friends and students, I asked them what her life mission and core teaching had been. Some talked about her compassion, others about her selfless service. There were miracle stories and humorous anecdotes. But this reflection about "becoming mother" stopped me short.

"Whoever we are, whether male or female," I recalled, trying to reconstruct as much as possible of my brief con-

versation with the young man, "we need a connection to
the primal energy that 'mother' ideally represents: generation, creativity, nurturance, protection, guidance, endurance,
receptivity, softness with strength." Without this connection we miss a full half of our heritage and thus subject our
own inner child to a life of deprivation. Without this connection we approach the world with one hand tied behind
our backs. And God knows the world is sorely in need of
conscious, two-handed parents in this critical time.

For many of us (male or female), therefore, mothering—in the way Dina spoke of it—doesn't come naturally.
More likely, we will have to labor to resurrect it, applying
conscious attention to experiencing ourselves in this way.
If we have never borne children in our own bodies, or
never had the opportunity to be responsible for children,
the notion of becoming "mother" in relationship to life may
remain even more remote—a good idea, but ungrounded in
the body.

Child-related loss can be a doorway into the clear per-
ception of that "motherless" or "mother-lacking" condition
that may lie at the root of much of our violence, separation,
and pain. Whether we are male or female, such grieving
can propel us into a domain of the feminine in which we are
more likely to surrender to life and receive from life in
general the gifts that are always being offered to us. Such
grieving will also leave us with a broken heart, but not
unhappy.

The open wound keeps the soul vulnerable to the
workings of the spirit. The memory of your lost child, or
your longing for one, can become for you an entryway into
the very heart of God. Susan and I wish you courage and
strength as you progress in your grief work, and hope you
have deep, abiding joy as the foundation of your life.

Finally, I am pleased to share with you a poem by
another poet-friend and colleague, Gregory Campbell. His

poem is really a prayer, and it speaks the sentiments of my heart.

THE PIED PIPER'S SONG

One by one,
all of my children were taken,
in the face of my tears,
from me.
Until all I had left was my face
and my anguish.
So, at last, I was forced finally to God.

And The Lord, in His Mercy,
saw I would rather have died.
So The Lord, in His Mercy, allowed that to happen.
He took my face, my form vanished,
and my anguish ended.
Now this Invincible Knowledge is mine:
  through the Truth of this death
    all children are mine.
      I am he
  who you knew in childhood as
    the Pied Piper.
  Your child will follow me.
    If you are wise
    you will follow your child.
This is the song I sing for them;
The only song I have:
    "I am going to follow God,
    I am going to follow God,
    I am not coming back. . ."

You can come too.
In the end
you must.

*   *   *

"... For he led us ... to a joyous land,
Joining the town and just at hand,
Where waters gushed and fruit-trees grew
And flowers put forth a fairer hue,
And everything was strange and new..." [1]

---

[1]Gregory Campbell, *"Yes, You Can Kiss My Bare Feet ..." our children are always saying—prose and poetry in celebration of our innate innocence* (Prescott, AZ: Hohm Press, 1987). Used with permission.

Bibliography and Selected Reading

GENERAL GRIEF

Bridges, Bill. *Transitions: Making Sense of Life's Changes.*
    Reading, MA: Addison-Wesley, 1980.
Levine, Stephen. *Healing Into Life and Death.*
    N.Y.: Bantam Publishing, 1987.
Kouri, Mary K. *Keys To Dealing With Loss of A Loved One.*
    Hauppauge, N.Y.: Barron's Educational Series, 1991.
Kubler-Ross, Elisabeth. *On Death and Dying.*
    NY: Macmillan, 1969.
    — *Living With Death And Dying.*
    NY: Macmillan, 1981.
Stearns, Ann Kaiser. *Living Through Personal Crisis.*
    NY: Ballantine Books, 1984.

MISCARRIAGE

Williamson, Walter. *Miscarriage: Sharing the Grief, Facing the Pain, Healing the Wounds.* New York: Walker and Company, 1987.

Ilse, Sherokee, and Burn, Linda H. *Miscarriage: A Shattered Dream.* Wintergreen Press, 1985.

DEATH AND CHILDREN

Kubler-Ross, Elisabeth. *On Children and Death.* NY: Macmillan, 1983.

Schiff, Harriet Sarnoff. *The Bereaved Parent.* NY: Penguin Books, 1977.

Von Schilling, Karin. *Where Are You?: Coming to Terms with the Death of My Child.* Hudson, N.Y.: Anthroposophic Press, Inc., 1988.

DEATH OF A BABY

Limbo, Rana I., and Wheeler, Sara R. *When A Baby Dies: A Handbook for Healing and Helping.* Holmen, WI: Harsand Press, 1988.

Davis, Deborah L. *Empty Cradle, Broken Heart: Surviving the Death of Your Baby.* Golden, CO: Fulcrum Publishing, 1991.

ABORTION

Nathanson, Sue. *Soul Crisis: One Woman's Journey Through Abortion to Renewal.* New York: NAL/Dutton, 1989.

ADOPTION

Arms, Suzanne. *Adoption: A Handful of Hope* . Berkeley,
CA: Celestial Arts, 1992.

MEN'S GRIEF

Knapp, Ronald J. *Beyond Endurance: When a Child Dies*.
New York: Schocken Books, Inc., 1986.
Staudacher, Carol. *Men and Grief*. Oakland, CA:
New Harbinger Publications, 1991.

CHILDREN WITH DISABILITIES

Buscaglia, Leo. *The Disabled and Their Parents—A
Counseling Challenge*. Thorofare, N.J.: Slack Inc.,
1983.
Featherstone, Helen. *A Difference in the Family—
Living with a Disabled Child*. New York:
Penguin Books, 1981.

CHILDREN OF DIVORCE

Berger, Stuart, M.D. *Divorce Without Victims—Helping
Children*. New York: Signet Books, 1986.
Despert, J. Louise, M.D. *Children of Divorce*. New York:
Doubleday and Co., 1953.
Mitchell, Ann. *Children In the Middle—Living Through
Divorce*. New York: Tavistock, 1985.
Wallerstein, Judith S., and Kelly, Joan Berlin. *Surviving
the Breakup—How Children and Parents Cope
With Divorce*. New York: Basic Books, 1980.

HEALING OUR CHILDHOOD LOSSES

Bradshaw, John. *Homecoming: Reclaiming and
    Championing Your Inner Child.* N.Y.: Bantam
    Publishing, 1990.
Capacchione, Lucia. *Recovery of Your Inner Child.*
    New York: Simon and Schuster, 1991.
Kunzman, Kristin. *The Healing Way: Adult Recovery from
    Childhood Sexual Abuse.* San Francisco, CA:
    Harper and Row, 1990.
Middleton-Moz, Jane, and Dwinell, Lori. *After the Tears:
    Reclaiming the Personal Losses of Childhood.*
    Pompano Beach, FL: Health Communications,
    1986.
Miller, Alice. *Banished Knowledge: Facing Childhood
    Injuries.* N.Y.: Bantam Publishing, 1990.
Stettbacher, J. Konrad. *Making Sense of Suffering.* N.Y.:
    Penguin Books, 1991.
Woodman, Marion. *Leaving My Father's House.*
    Boston, MA: Shambhala Publishing, 1992.

SELF-CARE AS YOU GRIEVE

Travis, John W., M.D., and Ryan, Regina Sara. *The Wellness
    Workbook.* Berkeley, CA: Ten Speed Press, 1988.
Thomas, Lalitha. *Ten Essential Herbs.* Prescott, AZ:
    Hohm Press, 1992.

WRITING AND JOURNALLING

Capacchione, Lucia. *The Creative Journal: The Art of
    Finding Yourself.* North Hollywood, CA:
    Newcastle Publishing Co., Inc., 1989.

—*The Power of Your Other Hand.* North Hollywood,
    CA: Newcastle Publishing Co., Inc., 1988.
Goldberg, Natalie. *Writing Down the Bones: Freeing The
    Writer Within.* Boston, MA: Shambhala, 1986.
Rainer, Tristine. *The New Diary.* Los Angeles, CA: J.P.
    Tarcher, Inc., 1978.

USING DREAMS

Kaplan-Williams, Strephon. *The Jungian-Senoi
        Dreamwork Manual.* Novato, CA: Journey Press,
        1988.
Johnson, Robert A. *Inner Work: Using Dreams and
        Active Imagination For Personal Growth.* San
        Francisco, CA: Harper and Row, Publishers, 1986.

CREATING RITUALS

Feinstein, David, and May, Peg Elliott. *Rituals for Living
        and Dying.* San Francisco, CA: HarperSanFrancisco,
        1990.

USING MUSIC

The music of the rock group "liars, gods, and beggars":
album suggestions, *Just Smoke, Lilith,* and *Eccentricities,
Idiosyncrasies, and Indiscretions.* Available from: LGB
Music, PO Box 4272, Prescott, AZ 86302 (602) 776-8259.
The music of Gabrielle Roth: album suggestions:
        Initiation, Rituals, and *Bones.* Available from: The
        Moving Center, PO Box 2034, Red Bank, NJ 07701,
        (212) 505-7928.

Resource Guide

The following selected list of national organizations is taken from the *Encyclopedia of Associations*, available at the public library. Each of these organizations has local chapters. To find one in your area, contact the national office, or consult your telephone directory under Social Services or Social Welfare. You can also find local groups by contacting your local hospital, church, or information and referral services.

ADOPTION

Planned Parenthood Federation of America (PPFA)
810 Seventh Ave.
New York, N.Y. 10019
(212) 541-7800

National Adoption Assistance Center
444 Lincoln Blvd. #107
Venice, CA 90291

Committee for Single Adoptive Parents (helping single people to adopt a child)
PO Box 15084
Chevy Chase, MD 20825
(202) 966-6367

The ALMA Society (helping adoptees and birth parents to find one another)
PO Box 154
Washington Bridge Station
New York, N.Y. 10033

SEXUAL ABUSE

Survivors of Incest Anonymous (Sexual Abuse) (SIA)
PO Box 21817
Baltimore, MD 21222-6817
(301) 282-3400

DEATH OF A CHILD

The Compassionate Friends (parents who have lost a child through death) (TCF)
PO Box 3696
Oak Brook, IL 60522-3696
(708) 990-0010

Sids Alliance
10500 Little Patuxent Pkway, No. 420
Columbia, MD 21044
(410) 964-8000

ABORTION COUNSELING

Planned Parenthood (see address above)

Birthright, United States of America (alternatives to abortion; private and interdenominational)
686 N. Broad St.
Woodbury, N.J. 08096
(609) 848-1819

MISCARRIAGE

Pregnancy and Infant Loss Center (PILC)
1421 E. Wayzata Blvd. #40
Wayzata, MN 55391
(612) 473-9372

CUSTODY

Fathers Are Forever (Custody Loss) (FAF)
PO Box 4804
Panorama City, CA 91412
(818) 566-3368
(800) 248-DADS

Mothers Without Custody (Custody Loss) (MWOC)
PO Box 27418
Houston, TX 77227
(800) 457-6962

INFERTILITY AND OPTIONS (ADOPTION)

National Infertility Network Exchange (NINE)
P.O. BOX 204
E. Meadow, N.Y. 11554
(516) 794-5772

RESOLVE (infertility issues)
PO Box 54214
Phoenix, AZ 85078
(602) 995-3933

Pregnancy and Infant Loss Center (PILC)
1421 E. Wayzata Blvd. #40
Wayzata, MN 55391
(612) 473-9372

We invite you to join with others in building a community of men and women dedicated to developing spiritual self-reliance and cooperative interaction.

The Stillpoint Institute was founded on the belief that the universal insight we want and need to heal and sustain our lives and life on the planet comes from a deeper connection to the God-force and through our personal spiritual work.

Our commitment at the Institute is to create an effective network of individuals and groups of people who are seeking to use the spiritual energy of Love to heal and help themselves and others.

If you are interested in learning more about Stillpoint Institute's outreach efforts and ways you can be part of this healing community, please write or call Stillpoint.

> Stillpoint Institute for Life Healing
> Meetinghouse Road
> P.O. Box 640
> Walpole, NH 03608
> 603-756-9281